Azure Serverless Computing Cookbook

Build applications hosted on serverless architecture using Azure Functions

Praveen Kumar Sreeram

BIRMINGHAM - MUMBAI

Azure Serverless Computing Cookbook

First published: August 2017

Production reference: 1160817

Published by Packt Publishing Ltd.
Livery Place
35 Livery Street
Birmingham
B3 2PB, UK.

ISBN 978-1-78839-082-8

www.packtpub.com

Credits

Author
Praveen Kumar Sreeram

Reviewer
Florian Klaffenbach

Commissioning Editor
Vijin Boricha

Acquisition Editor
Shrilekha Inani

Content Development Editor
Sweeny Dias

Technical Editor
Komal Karne

Copy Editor
Stuti Srivastava

Project Coordinator
Virginia Dias

Proofreader
Safis Editing

Indexer
Aishwarya Gangawane

Graphics
Kirk D'Penha

Production Coordinator
Aparna Bhagat

Foreword

It is my pleasure to write the foreword for *Azure Serverless Computing Cookbook* by Praveen Kumar Sreeram. Azure Functions is one of the key Platform as a service (PaaS) components from Microsoft and provides a rich experience for the event-driven, compute-on-demand programming model. To use Azure Functions, the user is not required to be a master of any specific programming language; rather, they can use their language of choice, such as C#, Node.js, JavaScript, PowerShell, and so on, to create highly scalable functions.

Azure Serverless Computing Cookbook shows the author's dedication and hard work to come out with a gem that will not only benefit developers and architects, but also enterprises that want to leverage serverless solutions in Azure. The author has thoroughly gone through each parameter and every consideration in tackling the concept of Azure Functions. You will surely like the way numerous code samples and use cases blend together to create a knowledge repository for you to start with cloud development on the go.

I would like to thank Packt, Mohd. Riyan Khan, and Shrilekha Inani for involving me in evaluating the content and giving me the opportunity to write this foreword.

Abhishek Kumar

Microsoft Azure MVP and Consultant – Datacom New Zealand

About the Author

Praveen Kumar Sreeram works as a Solution Architect at PennyWise Solutions (an Ogilvy and Mather Company). He has over 12 years of experience in the field of development, analysis, design, and delivery of applications of various technologies, including custom web development using ASP.NET and MVC to building mobile apps using the cross-platform technology Xamarin for domains such as insurance, telecom, and wireless expense management. He has been awarded two times as the Most Valuable Professional by one of the most leading social community websites, CSharpCorner, for his contributions toward writing articles and helping community members, mostly on Microsoft Azure. He is highly focused on learning about technology. He is an avid blogger who writes about his learning at his personal blog, called PraveenKumarSreeram and you can also follow him on twitter at @PrawinSreeram. His current focus is on analyzing business problems and providing technical solutions for various projects related to Microsoft Azure and Sitecore.

First of all, my thanks go to the great editorial team at Packt Publishing for identifying my potential and giving me the opportunity to write this book, especially Shrilekha Inani, Sweeny Dias, Komal Karne, Yogesh Mishra, and the whole team who encouraged me a lot. Without them, I couldn't have done it.

I would like to thank my current employer, PennyWise Solutions, all of my management team, especially the CTOs, Mr. Pavan Pochu and Mr. Arup Dutta, for guiding me all the way, and my lovely colleagues who encouraged me a lot.

I would like to thank my grandma Neelavatamma; dad, Kamalakar; mom, Seetha; my better half, Haritha; and my little princess, Rithwika; for being in my life and giving me courage all the time.

I would like to express my deepest gratitude to Medeme Narasimhulu and Medeme Saraswathi (my uncle and aunt) who have been supporting me and encouraging me right from my college days. Without them, I wouldn't have even become a software professional.

About the Reviewer

Florian Klaffenbach started his IT career in 2004 as a 1st and 2nd level IT support technician and IT salesman trainee for a B2B online shop. After that, he changed to a small company working as IT project manager for planning, implementing, and integrating from industrial plants and laundries into enterprise IT. After a few years, he changed course to Dell Germany. There, he started from scratch as an enterprise technical support analyst and later worked on a project to start Dell technical communities and support over social media in Europe and outside of the US. Currently, he works as a Technology Solutions Professional for Microsoft, specializing in hybrid Microsoft cloud infrastructured.

Additionally, he is active as a Microsoft blogger and lecturer. He blogs on his own page, Datacenter-Flo.de, and the Brocade Germany community. Together with a very good friend, he founded Windows Server User Group Berlin to create a network of Microsoft IT Pros in Berlin. Florian maintains a very tight network with many vendors such as Cisco, Dell, and Microsoft and several communities. This helps him grow his experience and get the best out of a solution for his customers. Since 2016, he has also been the Co-Chairman of the Azure community Germany. In April 2016, Microsoft awarded Florian the Microsoft Most Valuable Professional for Cloud and Datacenter Management. In 2017, after joining Microsoft, Florian became an MVP reconnect member.

Florian has worked for several companies and Microsoft partners such as Dell Germany, CGI Germany, and msg services ag. Now he has joined Microsoft Germany in a technical presales role and supports customers in getting started with hybrid cloud infrastructures and topics.

He has also worked on the following books:

- *Taking Control with System Center App Controller*
- *Microsoft Azure Storage Essentials*
- *Mastering Cloud Development using Microsoft Azure*
- *Mastering Microsoft Deployment Toolkit 2013*
- *Implementing Azure Design Patterns*
- *Windows Server 2016 Cookbook*
- *Mastering Active Directory*
- *Exchange PowerShell Cookbook*
- *Implementing Azure Solutions*

Acknowledgments

I want to thank Packt Publishing for giving me the chance to review the book as well as my employer and my family for being accommodating of the time investment I have made in this project. There is a special thanks I need to make to Virginia Dias from Packt. It is always awesome to be a reviewer on her projects, and it's a great pleasure to work with her.

www.PacktPub.com

For support files and downloads related to your book, please visit www.PacktPub.com. Did you know that Packt offers eBook versions of every book published, with PDF and ePub files available? You can upgrade to the eBook version at www.PacktPub.com and as a print book customer, you are entitled to a discount on the eBook copy. Get in touch with us at service@packtpub.com for more details. At www.PacktPub.com, you can also read a collection of free technical articles, sign up for a range of free newsletters and receive exclusive discounts and offers on Packt books and eBooks.

https://www.packtpub.com/mapt

Get the most in-demand software skills with Mapt. Mapt gives you full access to all Packt books and video courses, as well as industry-leading tools to help you plan your personal development and advance your career.

Why subscribe?

- Fully searchable across every book published by Packt
- Copy and paste, print, and bookmark content
- On demand and accessible via a web browser

Customer Feedback

Thanks for purchasing this Packt book. At Packt, quality is at the heart of our editorial process. To help us improve, please leave us an honest review on this book's Amazon page at https://www.amazon.com/dp/1788390822.

If you'd like to join our team of regular reviewers, you can e-mail us at customerreviews@packtpub.com. We award our regular reviewers with free eBooks and videos in exchange for their valuable feedback. Help us be relentless in improving our products!

Table of Contents

Preface

Microsoft provides a solution to easily run small segments of code in the cloud with Azure Functions. Azure Functions provides solutions for processing data, integrating systems, and building simple APIs and microservices.

The book starts with intermediate-level recipes on serverless computing along with some use cases on the benefits and key features of Azure Functions. Then, we'll deep dive into the core aspects of Azure Functions, such as the services it provides, how you can develop and write Azure Functions, and how to monitor and troubleshoot them.

Moving on, you'll get practical recipes on integrating DevOps with Azure Functions, and providing continuous deployment with Visual Studio Team Services. The book also provides hands-on steps and tutorials based on real-world serverless use cases to guide you through configuring and setting up your serverless environments with ease. Finally, you'll see how to manage Azure Functions, providing enterprise-level security and compliance to your serverless code architecture.

By the end of this book, you will have all the skills required to work with serverless code architectures, providing continuous delivery to your users.

What this book covers

Chapter 1, *Accelerate Your Cloud Application Development Using Azure Function Triggers and Bindings*, goes through how the Azure Functions Runtime provides templates that can be used to quickly integrate different Azure services for your application needs. It reduces all of the plumbing code so that you can focus on just your application logic. In this chapter, you will learn how to build web APIs and bindings related to Azure Storage Services.

Chapter 2, *Working with Notifications Using SendGrid and Twilio Services*, deals with how communication is one of the most critical part of any business requirement. In this chapter, you will learn how easy it is to connect your business requirements written in Azure Functions with the most popular communication services such as SendGrid (for email) and Twilio (for SMS).

Chapter 3, *Seemless Integration of Azure Functions with Other Azure Services*, discusses how Azure provides many connectors that you could leverage to integrate your business applications with other systems pretty easily. In this chapter, you will learn how to integrate Azure Functions with cognitive services, Logic Apps, and OneDrive.

Chapter 4, *Understanding the Integrated Developer Experience of Visual Studio Tools for Azure Functions*, builds on the previous chapters and teaches you how to develop Azure Functions using Visual Studio, which provides you many features such as Intellisense, local and remote debugging, and most of the regular development features.

Chapter 5, *Exploring Testing Tools for the Validation of Azure Functions*, helps you understand different tools and processes that help you streamline your development and quality control processes. You will also learn how to create loads using VSTS load testing and monitor the performance of VMs using the reports provided by Application Insights. Finally, you will also learn how to configure alerts that notify you when your apps are not responsive.

Chapter 6, *Monitoring and Troubleshooting Azure Serverless Services*, teaches you how to continuously monitor applications, analyze the performance, and review the logs to understand whether there are any issues that end users are facing. Azure provides us with multiple tools to achieve all the monitoring requirements, right from the development stage and the maintenance stage of the application.

Chapter 7, *Code Reusability and Refactoring the Code in Azure Functions*, helps you in understanding how to refactor your code and make use of classes for reusability in serverless architectures. You will also learn how to migrate legacy C# classes to Azure serverless functions.

Chapter 8, *Developing Reliable and Durable Serverless Applications Using Durable Functions*, shows you how to develop long-running, stateful solutions in serverless environments using Durable Functions, which has advanced features that have been released as an extension to Azure Functions.

Chapter 9, *Implement Best Practices for Azure Functions*, teaches a few of the best practices that one should follow to improve performance and security while working in Azure Functions.

Chapter 10, *Implement Continuous Integration and Deployment of Azure Functions Using Visual Studio Team Services*, helps you learn how to implement continuous integration and delivery of your Azure Functions code with the help of Visual Studio and VSTS.

What you need for this book

Prior knowledge and hands-on experience with core services of Microsoft Azure is required.

Who this book is for

If you are a cloud administrator, architect, or developer who wants to build scalable systems and deploy serverless applications with Azure Functions, then this book is for you.

Sections

In this book, you will find several headings that appear frequently (Getting ready, How to do it..., How it works..., There's more..., and See also). To give clear instructions on how to complete a recipe, we use these sections as follows:

Getting ready

This section tells you what to expect in the recipe, and describes how to set up any software or any preliminary settings required for the recipe.

How to do it...

This section contains the steps required to follow the recipe.

How it works...

This section usually consists of a detailed explanation of what happened in the previous section.

There's more...

This section consists of additional information about the recipe in order to make the reader more knowledgeable about the recipe.

See also

This section provides helpful links to other useful information for the recipe.

Conventions

In this book, you will find a number of text styles that distinguish between different kinds of information. Here are some examples of these styles and an explanation of their meaning. Code words in text, database table names, folder names, filenames, file extensions, pathnames, dummy URLs, user input, and Twitter handles are shown as follows: "For this example, I have used `RegisterUser` as the name of the Azure Function."

A block of code is set as follows:

```
public UserProfile(string lastName, string firstName)
        {
            this.PartitionKey = "p1";
            this.RowKey = Guid.NewGuid().ToString();;
        }
```

Any command-line input or output is written as follows:

```
Install-Package Microsoft.Azure.WebJobs.Extensions -Version 2.0.0
```

New terms and **important words** are shown in bold. Words that you see on the screen, for example, in menus or dialog boxes, appear in the text like this: "In the **SendGrid Email Delivery** blade, click on the **Create** button to navigate to **Create a New SendGrid Account**."

Warnings or important notes appear like this.

Tips and tricks appear like this.

Reader feedback

Feedback from our readers is always welcome. Let us know what you think about this book-what you liked or disliked. Reader feedback is important for us as it helps us develop titles that you will really get the most out of. To send us general feedback, simply e-mail feedback@packtpub.com, and mention the book's title in the subject of your message. If there is a topic that you have expertise in and you are interested in either writing or contributing to a book, see our author guide at www.packtpub.com/authors.

Customer support

Now that you are the proud owner of a Packt book, we have a number of things to help you to get the most from your purchase.

Downloading the example code

You can download the example code files for this book from your account at `www.packtpub.com`. If you purchased this book elsewhere, you can visit `www.packtpub.com/support`, and register to have the files e-mailed directly to you. You can download the code files by following these steps:

1. Log in or register to our website using your e-mail address and password.
2. Hover the mouse pointer on the **SUPPORT** tab at the top.
3. Click on **Code Downloads & Errata**.
4. Enter the name of the book in the **Search** box.
5. Select the book for which you're looking to download the code files.
6. Choose from the drop-down menu where you purchased this book from.
7. Click on **Code Download**.

You can also download the code files by clicking on the **Code Files** button on the book's webpage at the Packt Publishing website. This page can be accessed by entering the book's name in the **Search** box. Please note that you need to be logged in to your Packt account. Once the file is downloaded, please make sure that you unzip or extract the folder using the latest version of:

- WinRAR / 7-Zip for Windows
- Zipeg / iZip / UnRarX for Mac
- 7-Zip / PeaZip for Linux

The code bundle for the book is also hosted on GitHub at `https://github.com/PacktPublishing/Azure-Serverless-Computing-Cookbook`. We also have other code bundles from our rich catalog of books and videos available at `https://github.com/PacktPublishing/`. Check them out!

Downloading the color images of this book

We also provide you with a PDF file that has color images of the screenshots/diagrams used in this book. The color images will help you better understand the changes in the output. You can download this file from `https://www.packtpub.com/sites/default/files/downloads/AzureServerlessComputingCookbook_ColorImages.pdf`.

Errata

Although we have taken every care to ensure the accuracy of our content, mistakes do happen. If you find a mistake in one of our books-maybe a mistake in the text or the code-we would be grateful if you could report this to us. By doing so, you can save other readers from frustration and help us improve subsequent versions of this book. If you find any errata, please report them by visiting `http://www.packtpub.com/submit-errata`, selecting your book, clicking on the **Errata Submission Form** link, and entering the details of your errata. Once your errata are verified, your submission will be accepted and the errata will be uploaded to our website or added to any list of existing errata under the Errata section of that title. To view the previously submitted errata, go to `https://www.packtpub.com/books/content/support`, and enter the name of the book in the search field. The required information will appear under the **Errata** section.

Piracy

Piracy of copyrighted material on the Internet is an ongoing problem across all media. At Packt, we take the protection of our copyright and licenses very seriously. If you come across any illegal copies of our works in any form on the Internet, please provide us with the location address or website name immediately so that we can pursue a remedy. Please contact us at `copyright@packtpub.com` with a link to the suspected pirated material. We appreciate your help in protecting our authors and our ability to bring you valuable content.

Questions

If you have a problem with any aspect of this book, you can contact us at `questions@packtpub.com`, and we will do our best to address the problem.

1
Accelerate Your Cloud Application Development Using Azure Function Triggers and Bindings

In this chapter, we will cover the following recipes:

- Building a backend Web API using HTTP triggers
- Persisting employee details using Azure Storage table output bindings
- Saving the profile images to Queues using Queue output bindings
- Storing the image in Azure Blob storage
- Cropping an image using ImageResizer trigger

Introduction

Every software application needs backend components that are responsible for taking care of the business logic and storing the data into some kind of storage such as database, filesystem, and so on. Each of these backend components could be developed using different technologies. Azure serverless technology also allows us to develop these backend APIs using Azure Functions.

Azure Functions provide many out-of-the-box templates that solves most of the common problems such as connecting to storage, building Web APIs, cropping the images, and so on. In this chapter, we will learn how to use these built-in templates. Along with learning the concepts related to Azure serverless computing, we will also try to implement a solution to a basic domain problem of creating components required for any organization to manage the internal employee information.

Below is a simple diagram that helps you understand what we will be going to achieve in this chapter:

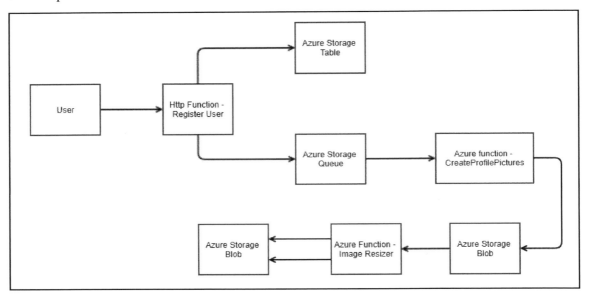

Building a backend Web API using HTTP triggers

We will use Azure serverless architecture for building a Web API using HTTP triggers. These HTTP triggers could be consumed by any frontend application that is capable of making HTTP calls.

Getting ready

Let's start our journey of understanding Azure serverless computing using Azure Functions by creating a basic backend Web API that responds to HTTP requests:

- Please refer to the URL https://azure.microsoft.com/en-in/free/?wt.mc_id= AID607363_SEM_8y6Q27AS for creating a free Azure Account.
- Also, visit https://docs.microsoft.com/en-us/azure/azure-functions/ functions-create-function-app-portal to understand the step by step process of creating a function app and https://docs.microsoft.com/en-us/azure/ azure-functions/functions-create-first-azure-function to create a function. While creating a function, a Storage Account is also created for storing all the files. Please remember the name of the Storage Account which will be used later in the other chapters.

 We will be using C# as the programming language throughout the book.

How to do it...

1. Navigate to the **Function App** listing page. Choose the function app in which you would like to add a new function.
2. Create a new function by clicking on the + icon as shown in the following screenshot:

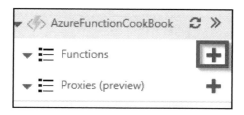

3. If you have created a brand new function, then clicking on the **+** icon in the preceding step, you would see the **Get started quickly with a premade function** page. Please click on the **create your own custom functions** link to navigate to the page where you can see all the built-in templates for creating your Azure Functions.

4. In the **Choose a template below or go to the quickstart** section, choose **HTTPTrigger-CSharp** as shown in the following screenshot to create a new HTTP trigger function:

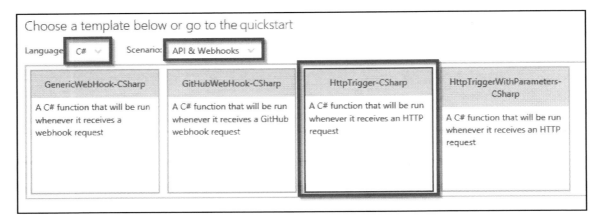

5. Provide a meaningful name. For this example, I have used `RegisterUser` as the name of the Azure Function.

6. In the **Authorization level** drop-down, choose the **Anonymous** option as shown in the following screenshot. We will learn more about the all the authorization levels in `Chapter 9`, *Implement Best Practices for Azure Functions*:

7. Once you provide the name and choose the **Authorization level,** click on **Create** button to create the HTTP trigger function.

8. As soon as you create the function, all the required code and configuration files will be created automatically and the `run.csx` file will be opened for you to edit the code. Remove the default code and replace it with the following code:

```
using System.Net;
public static async Task<HttpResponseMessage>
Run(HttpRequestMessage req, TraceWriter log)
{
    string firstname=null,lastname = null;
    dynamic data = await req.Content.ReadAsAsync<object>();
    firstname = firstname ?? data?.firstname;
    lastname = data?.lastname;
    return (lastname + firstname) == null ?
     req.CreateResponse(HttpStatusCode.BadRequest,
     "Please pass a name on the query string or in the
     request body") :
     req.CreateResponse(HttpStatusCode.OK, "Hello " +
     firstname + " " + lastname);
}
```

9. Save the changes by clicking on the **Save** button available just above the code editor.

10. Let's try to test the `RegisterUser` function using the **Test** console. Click on the tab named **Test** as shown in the following screenshot to open the **Test** console:

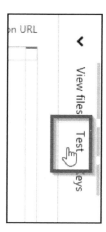

11. Enter the values for `firstname` and `lastname`, in the **Request body** section as shown in the following screenshot:

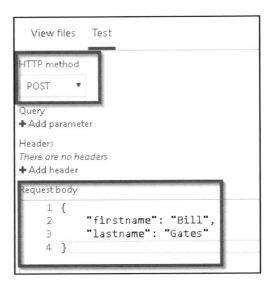

Please make sure you select **POST** in the **HTTP method** drop-down.

12. Once you have reviewed the input parameters, click on the **Run** button available at the bottom of the **Test** console as shown in the following screenshot:

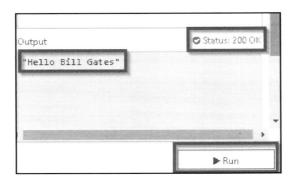

13. If the input request workload is passed correctly with all the required parameters, you will see a **Status 200 OK,** and the output in the **Output** window will be as shown in the preceding screenshot.

How it works...

We have created the first basic Azure Function using HTTP triggers and made a few modifications to the default code. The code just accepts `firstname` and `lastname` parameters and prints the name of the end user with a `Hello {firstname} {lastname}` message as a response. We have also learnt how to test the HTTP trigger function right from the Azure Management portal.

 For the sake of simplicity, I didn't perform validations of the input parameter. Please make sure that you validate all the input parameters in your applications running on your production environment.

See also

- The *Enabling authorization for function apps* recipe in `Chapter 9`, *Implement Best Practices for Azure Functions*

Persisting employee details using Azure Storage table output bindings

In the previous recipe, you have learnt how to create an HTTP trigger and accept the input parameters. Let's now work on something interesting, that is, where you store the input data into a persistent medium. Azure Functions supports us to store data in many ways. For this example, we will store the data in Azure Table storage.

Getting ready

In this recipe, you will learn how easy it is to integrate an HTTP trigger and the **Azure Table storage** service using output bindings. The Azure HTTP trigger function receives the data from multiple sources and stores the user profile data in a storage table named `tblUserProfile`.

- For this recipe, we will use the same HTTP trigger that we have created in our previous recipe.

- We will be using **Azure Storage Explorer** which is a tool that helps us to work with the data stored in Azure Storage account. You can download it from `http:/` `/storageexplorer.com/`.
- You can learn more about Connect to the Storage Account using Azure Storage Explorer at `https://docs.microsoft.com/en-us/azure/vs-azure-tools-` `storage-manage-with-storage-explorer`

How to do it...

1. Navigate to the **Integrate** tab of the `RegisterUser` HTTP trigger function.
2. Click on the **New Output** button and select **Azure Table Storage** then click on the **Select** button:

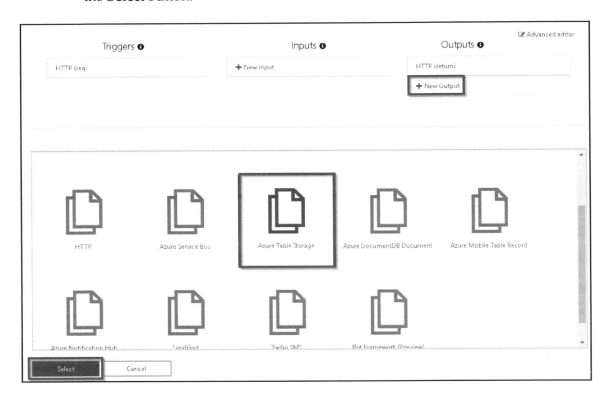

3. Once you click on the **Select** button in the previous step, you will be prompted to choose the following settings of the Azure Table storage output bindings:

- **Table parameter name**: This is the name of the parameter that you will be using in the `Run` method of the Azure Function. For this example, please provide `objUserProfileTable` as the value.
- **Table name**: A new table in the Azure Table storage will be created to persist the data. If the table doesn't exist already, Azure will automatically create one for you! For this example, please provide `tblUserProfile` as the table name.
- **Storage account connection**: If you don't see the **Storage account connection** string, click on the **new** (shown in the following screenshot) to create a new one or to choose an existing storage account.
- The Azure Table storage output bindings should be as shown in the following screenshot:

4. Click on **Save** to save the changes.

5. Navigate to the code editor by clicking on the function name and paste the following code:

```
#r "Microsoft.WindowsAzure.Storage"
using System.Net;
using Microsoft.WindowsAzure.Storage.Table;

public static async Task<HttpResponseMessage>
Run(HttpRequestMessage req,TraceWriter
log,CloudTable objUserProfileTable)
{
    dynamic data = await
     req.Content.ReadAsAsync<object>();
    string firstname= data.firstname;
    string lastname=data.lastname;

    UserProfile objUserProfile = new UserProfile(firstname,
     lastname);
    TableOperation objTblOperationInsert =
     TableOperation.Insert(objUserProfile);
    objUserProfileTable.Execute(objTblOperationInsert);
    return req.CreateResponse(HttpStatusCode.OK,
     "Thank you for Registering..");
}

public class UserProfile : TableEntity
{
    public UserProfile(string lastName, string firstName)
    {
        this.PartitionKey = "p1";
        this.RowKey = Guid.NewGuid().ToString();;
        this.FirstName = firstName;
        this.LastName = lastName;
    }
    public UserProfile() { }
    public string FirstName { get; set; }
    public string LastName { get; set; }
}
```

6. Let's execute the function by clicking on the **Run** button of the **Test** tab by passing `firstname` and `lastname` parameters in the **Request body** as shown in the following screenshot:

7. If everything went well, you should get a **Status 200 OK** message in the **Output** box as shown in the preceding screenshot. Let's navigate to Azure Storage Explorer and view the table storage to see if the table named `tblUserProfile` was created successfully:

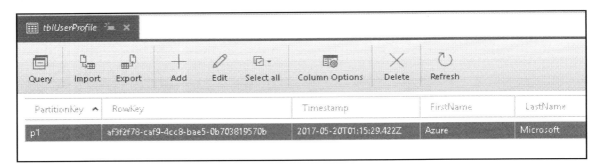

How it works...

Azure Functions allows us to easily integrate with other Azure services just by adding an output binding to the trigger. For this example, we have integrated the HTTP trigger with the Azure Storage table binding and also configured the Azure Storage account by providing the storage connection string and the Azure Storage table name in which we would like to create a record for each of the HTTP requests received by the HTTP trigger.

We have also added an additional parameter for handling the table storage named `objUserProfileTable`, of type `CloudTable`, to the `Run` method. We can perform all the operations on the Azure Table storage using `objUserProfileTable`.

 For the sake of explanation the input parameters are not validated in the code sample. However, in your production environment, it's important that you should validate them before storing in in any kind of persist medium.

We have also created an object of `UserProfile`, and filled it with the values received in the request object, and then passed it to a table operation. You can learn more about handling operations on Azure Table storage service from the URL `https://docs.microsoft.com/en-us/azure/storage/storage-dotnet-how-to-use-tables`.

Understanding more about Storage Connection

When you create a new storage connection (please refer to the third step of the *How to do it...* section of this recipe) a new **App settings** will be created as shown in the following screenshot:

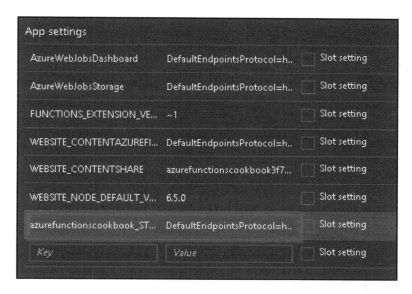

You can navigate to the **App settings** by clicking on **Application settings** of the **Platform features** tab as shown in the following screenshot:

What is Azure Table storage service?

Azure Table storage service is a NoSQL key-value persistent medium for storing semi-structured data. You can learn more about the same at `https://azure.microsoft.com/en-in/services/storage/tables/`.

Partition key and row key

The primary key of Azure Table storage tables has two parts as follows:

- **Partition key**: Azure Table storage records are classified and organized into partitions. Each record located in a partition will have the same partition key (p1 in our example).
- **Row key**: A unique value should be assigned for each of the rows.

 A clustered index will be created with the values of the partition key and row key to improve the query performance.

There's more...

Following is the very first line of the code in this recipe:

```
#r "Microsoft.WindowsAzure.Storage"
```

The preceding line of code instructs the function runtime to include a reference to the specified library to the current context.

Saving the profile images to Queues using Queue output bindings

In the previous recipe, you have learnt how to receive two string parameters `firstname` and `lastname` in the **Request body,** and store them in the Azure Table storage. In this recipe, you will learn how to receive a URL of an image and save the same in the Blob container of an Azure Storage account.

We could have processed the downloaded user profile image in the recipe *Persisting employee details using Azure Storage table output bindings*. However, keeping in mind the size of the profile pictures, the processing of images on the fly in the HTTP requests might hinder the performance of the function. For that reason, we will just grab the URL of the profile picture and store it in Queue, and later we can process the image and store it in the Blob.

Getting ready

We will be updating the code of the `RegisterUser` function that we have used in the previous recipes.

How to do it...

1. Navigate to the **Integrate** tab of the `RegisterUser` HTTP trigger function.
2. Click on the **New Output** button and select **Azure Queue Storage** then click on the **Select** button.
3. Provide the following parameters in the **Azure Queue Storage output** settings:
   - **Queue name**: Set the value of the Queue name as `userprofileimagesqueue`
   - **Storage account connection**: Please make sure that you select the right storage account in the **Storage account connection** field
   - **Message parameter name**: Set the name of the parameter to `objUserProfileQueueItem` which will be used in the `Run` method
4. Click on **Save** to the create the new output binding.

5. In this recipe, we will look at another approach of grabbing the request parameters for which we will use the **Newtonsoft.JSON** library to parse the JSON data. Let's navigate to the **View files** tab as shown in the following screenshot:

6. As shown in the preceding screenshot, click on **Add** to add a new file. Please make sure that you name it as `project.json` as shown in the preceding screenshot.
7. Once the file is created, add the following code to the `project.json` file. The following code adds the reference of the `Newtonsoft.Json` library.

```
{
"frameworks" : {
    "net46": {
        "dependencies":{
            "Newtonsoft.Json" : "10.0.2"
            }
        }
    }
}
```

8. Navigate back to the code editor by clicking on the function name (`RegisterUser` in this example) and paste the following code:

```
#r "Microsoft.WindowsAzure.Storage"
using System.Net;
using Microsoft.WindowsAzure.Storage.Table;
using Newtonsoft.Json;
```

```csharp
public static void Run(HttpRequestMessage req,
                       TraceWriter log,
                       CloudTable
                       objUserProfileTable,
                       out string
                       objUserProfileQueueItem
                       )
{
    var inputs = req.Content.ReadAsStringAsync().Result;
    dynamic inputJson = JsonConvert.DeserializeObject<dynamic>
      (inputs);
    string firstname= inputJson.firstname;
    string lastname=inputJson.lastname;
    string profilePicUrl = inputJson.ProfilePicUrl;

    objUserProfileQueueItem = profilePicUrl;
    UserProfile objUserProfile = new UserProfile(firstname,
      lastname, profilePicUrl);
    TableOperation objTblOperationInsert =
      TableOperation.Insert(objUserProfile);
    objUserProfileTable.Execute(objTblOperationInsert);
}

public class UserProfile : TableEntity
{
    public UserProfile(string lastname, string firstname,
      string profilePicUrl)
    {
        this.PartitionKey = "p1";
        this.RowKey = Guid.NewGuid().ToString();
        this.FirstName = firstname;
        this.LastName = lastname;
        this.ProfilePicUrl = profilePicUrl;
    }
    public UserProfile() { }
    public string FirstName { get; set; }
    public string LastName { get; set; }
    public string ProfilePicUrl {get; set;}
}
```

9. Click on **Save** to save the code changes in the code editor of the run.csx file.

10. Let's test the code by adding another parameter `ProfilePicUrl` to the **Request body** shown as follows then click on the **Run** button in the **Test** tab of the Azure Function code editor window: The image used in the below JSON might not exist when you are reading this book. So, Please make sure that you provide a valid URL of the image.

```
{
    "firstname": "Bill",
    "lastname": "Gates",
  "ProfilePicUrl":"https://upload.wikimedia.org/wikipedia/
    commons/1/19/Bill_Gates_June_2015.jpg"
}
```

11. If everything goes fine you will see the **Status : 200 OK** message, then the image URL that you have passed as an input parameter in the **Request body** will be created as a Queue message in the Azure Storage Queue service. Let's navigate to Azure Storage Explorer, and view the Queue named `userprofileimagesqueue`, which is the Queue name that we have provided in the *Step 3*. Following is the screenshot of the Queue message that was created:

How it works...

In this recipe, we have added Queue message output binding and made the following changes to the code:

- Added a reference to the `Newtonsoft.Json` NuGet library in the `project.json` file
- Added a new parameter named `out string objUserProfileQueueItem` which is used to bind the URL of the profile picture as a Queue message content
- We have also made the `Run` method synchronous by removing async as it doesn't allow us to have `out` parameters

There's more...

The `project.json` file contains all the references of the external libraries that we may use in the Azure Function.

 At the time of writing, Azure Function Runtime only supports .NET Framework 4.6.

See also

* The *Persisting employee details using Azure Storage table Output Bindings* recipe

Storing the image in Azure Blob storage

Let's learn how to invoke an Azure Function when a new queue item is added to the Azure Storage Queue service. Each message in the Queue is the URL of the profile picture of a user which will be processed by the Azure Functions and will be stored as a Blob in the Azure Storage Blob service.

Getting ready

In the previous recipe, we have learnt how to create Queue output bindings. In this recipe, you will grab the URL from the Queue, create a byte array, and then write it to a Blob.

This recipe is a continuation of the previous recipes. Please make sure that you implement them.

How to do it...

1. Create a new Azure Function by choosing the **QueueTrigger-C#** from the templates.
2. Provide the following details after choosing the template:
   - **Name your function:** Please provide a meaningful name such as `CreateProfilePictures`.
   - **Queue name**: Name of the Queue which should be monitored by the Azure Function. Our previous recipe created a new item for each of the valid requests coming to the HTTP trigger (named `RegisterUser`) into the `userprofileimagesqueue` Queue. For each new entry of a queue message to this Queue storage, the `CreateProfilePictures` trigger will be executed automatically.
   - **Storage account connection**: Connection of the storage account where the Queues are located.
3. Review all the details, and click on **Create** to create the new function.
4. Navigate to **Integrate** tab then click on **New Output** then choose **Azure Blob Storage** then click on the **Select** button.
5. In the **Azure Blob Storage output** section, provide the following:
   - **Blob parameter name**: Set it to `outputBlob`
   - **Path**: Set it to `userprofileimagecontainer/{rand-guid}`
   - **Storage account connection**: Choose the storage account where you would like to save the Blobs:

6. Once you provide all the preceding details, click on the **Save** button to save all the changes.

7. Replace the default code of the `run.csx` file with the following code:

```
using System;
public static void Run(Stream outputBlob,string myQueueItem,
 TraceWriter log)
{
    byte[] imageData = null;
    using (var wc = new System.Net.WebClient())
    {
        imageData = wc.DownloadData(myQueueItem);
    }
outputBlob.WriteAsync(imageData,0,imageData.Length);
}
```

8. Click on the **Save** button to save the changes.

9. Let's go back to the `RegisterUser` function and test it by providing `firstname`, `lastname`, and `ProfilePicUrl` fields as we did in the *Saving the profile images to Queues using Queue output bindings* recipe.

10. Now, navigate to the Azure Storage Explorer, and look at the Blob container `userprofileimagecontainer`. You will find a new Blob as shown in the following screenshot:

11. You can view the image in any tool (such as MS Paint or Internet Explorer).

How it works...

We have created a Queue trigger that gets executed as and when a new message arrives in the Queue. Once it finds a new Queue message, then it reads the message, and as we know the message is a URL of a profile picture. The function makes a web client request and downloads the image data in the form of byte array, and then writes the data into the Blob which is configured as an output Blob

There's more...

The parameter `rand-guid`, will generate a new GUID and is assigned to the Blob that gets created each time the trigger is fired.

It is mandatory to specify the Blob container name in the **Path** parameter of the Blob storage output binding while configuring the Blob storage output. Azure Functions creates one automatically if it doesn't exist.

You can use Queue messages only when you would like to store messages which are up to 64 KB. If you would like to store the messages greater than 64 KB, you need to use the Azure Service Bus.

See also...

- The *Building a backend Web API using HTTP triggers* recipe
- The *Persisting employee details using Azure Storage table output bindings* recipe
- The *Saving the profile images to Queues using Queue output bindings* recipe
- The *Storing the image in Azure Blob storage* recipe

Cropping an image using ImageResizer trigger

In the recent times, with the evolution of smart phones with high-end cameras, it's easy to capture a high-quality picture of huge sizes. It's good to have good quality pictures to refresh our memories. However, as an application developer or administrator, it would be a pain to manage the storage when your website is popular and you expect most of the users to get registered with a high-quality profile picture. So, it makes sense to use some libraries that could reduce the size of the high-quality images and crop them without losing the aspect ratio so that the quality of the image doesn't get reduced.

In this recipe, we will learn how to implement the functionality of cropping the image and reducing the size without losing the quality using one of the built-in Azure Function templates named `ImageResizer`.

Getting ready

In this recipe, you will learn how to use a library named `ImageResizer`. We will be using the library for resizing the image with the required dimensions. For the sake of simplicity, we will crop the image to the following sizes:

- Medium with 200*200 pixels
- Small with 100*100 pixels

How to do it...

1. Create a new Azure Function by choosing the **Samples** in the **Scenario** drop-down as shown in the following screenshot:

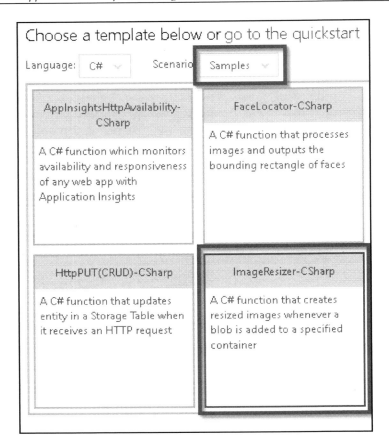

2. Select the **ImageResizer-CSharp** template as shown in the preceding screenshot.

3. Once you have selected the template, the portal prompts you to choose the following parameters:

   - **Name your Function**: Provide a meaningful name. For this example, I have provided `CropProfilePictures`.

   - **Azure Blob Storage trigger (image)**:
     - **Path**: Provide the path of the container (in our case `userprofileimagecontainer`) which contains all the blobs that are created by the Queue trigger. `CreateProfilePictures` in the previous recipe
     - **Storage account connection**: Select the connection string of the storage account where the container and Blobs are stored

- **Azure Blob Storage output (imageMedium)**:
  - **Path**: Please provide the name of the container where the resized images of size medium 200*200 are to be stored. In this case, `userprofileimagecontainer-md`.
  - **Storage account connection**: Select the connection string of the storage account where the Blobs are stored.
- **Azure Blob Storage output (imageSmall)**:
  - **Path**: Please provide the name of the container where the resized images of size small 100*100 are to be stored. In this case, `userprofileimagecontainer-sm`.
  - **Storage account connection**: Select the connection string of the storage account where the Blobs are stored.

4. Review all the details and click on **Create** as shown in the following screenshot:

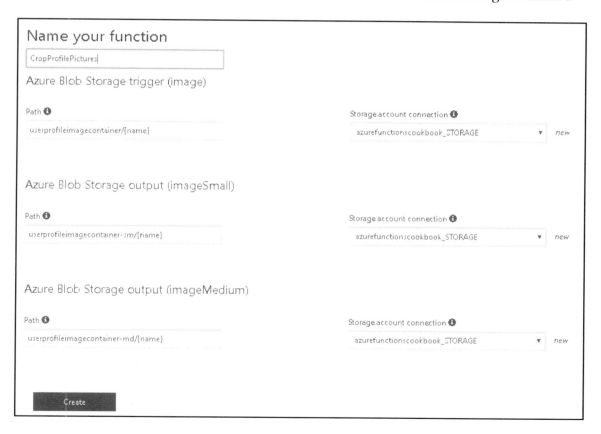

5. Fortunately, the `ImageResizer` Azure Function template provides most of the necessary code for our requirement of resizing the image. I just made a few minor tweaks. Replace the default code with the following code and the code should be self-explanatory:

```
using ImageResizer;

public static void Run(
   Stream image, Stream imageSmall, Stream imageMedium)
   {
      var imageBuilder = ImageResizer.ImageBuilder.Current;
      var size = imageDimensionsTable[ImageSize.Small];
      imageBuilder.Build(image, imageSmall, new ResizeSettings
        (size.Item1, size.Item2, FitMode.Max, null), false);
      image.Position = 0;
      size = imageDimensionsTable[ImageSize.Medium];
      imageBuilder.Build(image, imageMedium, new ResizeSettings
        (size.Item1, size.Item2, FitMode.Max, null), false);
   }

public enum ImageSize
{
    Small, Medium
}

private static Dictionary<ImageSize, Tuple<int, int>>
 imageDimensionsTable = new Dictionary<ImageSize, Tuple<int,
 int>>()
{
    { ImageSize.Small, Tuple.Create(100, 100) },
    { ImageSize.Medium, Tuple.Create(200, 200) }
};
```

6. Let's run a test on the `RegisterUser` function by submitting a sample request with `firstname`, `lastname`, and a `ProfilePicUrl`. I have used the same inputs that we have used in our previous recipes.

7. In the Azure Storage Explorer, I can see two new Blob containers `userprofileimagecontainer-md` and `userprofileimagecontainer-sm` as shown in the following screenshot:

8. I can even view the corresponding cropped versions in each of those containers. Following are the three versions of the image that we have used as input:

How it works...

We have created a new function using one of the samples named `ImageResizer` that the Azure Function template provides.

The `ImageResizer` template takes input from `userprofileimagecontainer` Blob container where the original Blobs reside. Whenever a new Blob is created in the `userprofileimagecontainer` Blob, the function will create two resized versions in each of the `userprofileimagecontainer-md` and `userprofileimagecontainer-sm` containers automatically.

Following is a simple diagram that shows how the execution of the functions is triggered like a chain:

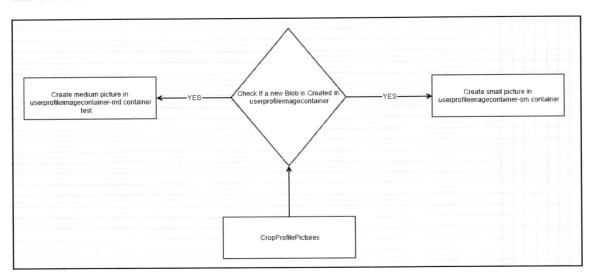

See also

- The *Building a backend Web API using HTTP triggers* recipe
- The *Persisting employee details using Azure Storage table output bindings* recipe
- The *Saving profile picture path to Azure Storage Queues using Queue output bindings* recipe
- The *Storing the image in Azure Blob storage* recipe

2
Working with Notifications Using SendGrid and Twilio Services

In this chapter, we will look at the following:

- Sending an email notification to the administrator of the website using the SendGrid service
- Sending an email notification to the end user dynamically
- Implementing email logging in the Blob storage
- Modifying the email content to include an attachment
- Sending SMS notification to the end user using the Twilio service

Introduction

For every business application to run it's business operations smoothly, one of the key features is to have a reliable communication system between the business and the customers. The communication channel might be two-way, either sending a message to the administrators managing the application or sending alerts to the customers via emails or SMS to their mobile phones.

Azure has integrations with two popular communication services named SendGrid for emails and Twilio for working with SMS. In this chapter, we will be using both the communication services to understand how to leverage their basic services to send messages between the business administrators and the end users.

Sending an email notification to the administrator of the website using the SendGrid service

In this recipe, you will learn how to create a SendGrid output binding and send an email notification to the administrator with static content. In general, there would be only administrators, so we will be hardcoding the email address of the administrator in the **To address** field of the **SendGrid output (message)** binding.

Getting ready

We will perform the following steps before moving to the next section:

1. Create a SendGrid account API key from the Azure Management portal.
2. Generate an API key from the SendGrid portal.

Creating a SendGrid account

1. Navigate to Azure Management portal and create a **SendGrid Email Delivery** account by searching for it in the Marketplace, as shown in the following screenshot:

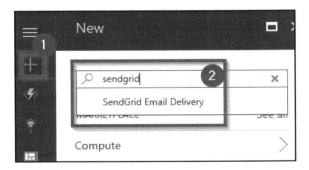

2. In the **SendGrid Email Delivery** blade, click on the **Create** button to navigate to **Create a New SendGrid Account**. Select **free** in **Pricing tier** and provide all the other details and click on the **Create** button, as shown in the following screenshot:

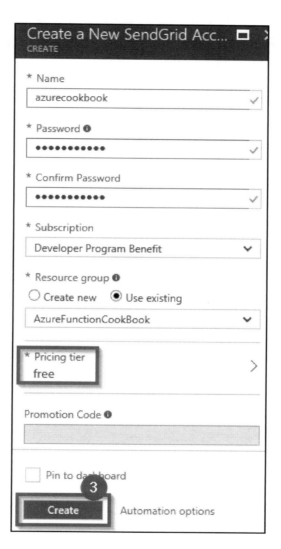

3. Once the account is created successfully, navigate to **SendGrid Accounts**. You can use the search box available on the top, as shown in the following screenshot:

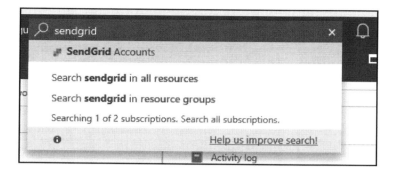

4. Navigate to **Settings**, choose **Configurations** , and grab **Username** and **SmtpServer** from the **Configurations** blade, as shown in the following screenshot:

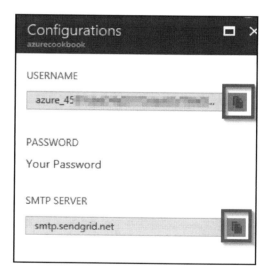

Generating the SendGrid API key

1. In order to utilize the SendGrid account by the Azure Functions runtime, we need to provide the SendGrid API key as input to the Azure Functions. You can generate an API key from the SendGrid portal. Let's navigate to the SendGrid portal by clicking on the **Manage** button in the **Essentials** blade of **SendGrid Account**, as shown in the following screenshot:

2. In the SendGrid portal, click on **API Keys** under the **Settings** section of the left-hand side menu, as shown in the following screenshot:

3. In the **API Keys** page, click on **Create API Key**, as shown in the following screenshot:

4. In the **Create API Key** popup, provide a name and choose **API Key Permissions** and click on the **Create & View** button.

5. After a moment, you will be able to see the API key. Click on the key to copy it to the clipboard, as shown in the following screenshot:

Configuring the SendGrid API key with the Azure Function app

1. Create a new **App settings** in the Azure Function app by navigating to the **Application settings** blade under the **Platform features** section, of the function app, as shown in the following screenshot:

2. Click on the **Save** button after adding the **App settings** in the preceding step.

How to do it...

1. Navigate to the **Integrate** tab of the `RegisterUser` function and click on the **New Output** button to add a new output binding.
2. Choose the **SendGrid** binding and click on the **Select** button to add the binding.
3. Provide the following parameters in the **SendGrid output (message)** binding:
   - **Message parameter name**: Leave the default value, which is `message`. We will be using this parameter in the `Run` method in a moment.
   - **SendGrid API Key**: Provide the **App settings** key that you have created in **Application settings**.
   - **To address**: Provide the email address of the administrator.
   - **From address**: Provide the email address from where you would like to send the email. In general, it would be something like `donotreply@example.com`.
   - **Message subject**: Provide the subject that you would like to have in the email subject.
   - **Message Text**: Provide the email body text that you would like to have in the email body.
4. This is how the **SendGrid output (message)** binding should look like after providing all the fields:

5. Once you review the values, click on **Save** to save the changes.

6. Navigate to the `Run` method and make the following changes:
   - Add a new reference for SendGrid and also the namespace `SendGrid.Helpers.Mail`.
   - Add a new out parameter message of type `Mail`.
   - Create an object of type `Mail`. We will understand how to use this object in the next recipe.

7. The following is the complete code of the `Run` method:

```
#r "Microsoft.WindowsAzure.Storage"
#r "SendGrid"

using System.Net;
using SendGrid.Helpers.Mail;
using Microsoft.WindowsAzure.Storage.Table;
using Newtonsoft.Json;
public static void Run(HttpRequestMessage req,
                       TraceWriter log,
                       CloudTable
                       objUserProfileTable,
                       out string
                       objUserProfileQueueItem,
                       out Mail message
                       )
{
    var inputs =
    req.Content.ReadAsStringAsync().Result;
    dynamic inputJson =
    JsonConvert.DeserializeObject<dynamic>
    (inputs);
    string firstname= inputJson.firstname;
    string lastname=inputJson.lastname;
    string profilePicUrl =
    inputJson.ProfilePicUrl;

    objUserProfileQueueItem = profilePicUrl;

    UserProfile objUserProfile = new
    UserProfile(firstname, lastname);
    TableOperation objTblOperationInsert =
    TableOperation.Insert(objUserProfile);
    objUserProfileTable.Execute
    (objTblOperationInsert);
    message = new Mail();
}
```

```
public class UserProfile : TableEntity
{
    public UserProfile(string lastName, string
    firstname,string profilePicUrl)
    {
        this.PartitionKey = "p1";
        this.RowKey = Guid.NewGuid().ToString();;
        this.FirstName = firstName;
        this.LastName = lastName;
        this.ProfilePicUrl = profilePicUrl;
    }
    public UserProfile() { }
    public string FirstName { get; set; }
    public string LastName { get; set; }
    public string ProfilePicUrl {get; set;}
}
```

8. Now, let's test the functionality of sending the email by navigating to the
   RegisterUser function and submitting a request with the some test values, as
   follows:

```
{
    "firstname": "Bill",
    "lastname": "Gates",
"ProfilePicUrl":"https://upload.wikimedia.org/
 wikipedia/commons/thumb/1/19/
 Bill_Gates_June_2015.jpg/220px-
 Bill_Gates_June_2015.jpg"
}
```

How it works...

The aim of this recipe is to send a notification via email to an administrator, updating that a
new registration got created successfully.

We have used the one of the Azure Function experimental templates named SendGrid as a
Simple Mail Transfer Protocol (SMTP) server to send the emails by hardcoding the
following properties in the **SendGrid output (message)** bindings:

- From the email address
- To the email address
- Subject of the email
- Body of the email

SendGrid output (message) bindings will use the API key provided in **App settings** to invoke the required APIs of the `SendGrid` library to send the emails.

See also

- The *Sending an email notification to the end user dynamically* recipe in this chapter

Sending an email notification to the end user dynamically

In the previous recipe, we hard coded most of the attributes related to sending an email to an administrator as there would be just one administrator. In this recipe, we will modify the previous recipe that sends emails to the user itself that sends a `Thank you for registration` email.

Getting ready

Make sure that the following are configured properly:

- The SendGrid account has been created and an API key is generated in the SendGrid portal
- An **App settings** is created in the **Application settings** of the function app
- The **App settings** key is configured in the **SendGrid output (message)** bindings

How to do it...

1. Navigate to the `RegisterUser` function and make the following changes.
2. Add a new string variable that accepts new input parameter named `email` from the `request` object:

    ```
    string firstname= inputJson.firstname;
    string lastname=inputJson.lastname;
    string profilePicUrl = inputJson.ProfilePicUrl;
    string email = inputJson.email;
    ```

```
UserProfile objUserProfile = new
 UserProfile(firstname,lastname,profilePicUrl,email);
```

3. Add the following code immediately after instantiating the message object:

```
message = new Mail();
message.Subject = "New User got registered
 successfully.";
message.From = new Email("donotreply@example.com");
message.AddContent(new Content("text/html","Thank you so much
 for getting registered to our site."));

Personalization personalization = new Personalization();
personalization.AddTo(new Email(email));
message.AddPersonalization(personalization);
....
....
....

public class UserProfile : TableEntity
{
    public UserProfile(string lastName, string firstName,string
     profilePicUrl,string email)
    {
       ....
       ....
       this.ProfilePicUrl = profilePicUrl;
       this.Email = email;
    }
       ....
       ....
    public string ProfilePicUrl {get; set;}
    public string Email  { get; set; }
}
```

Instead of hardcoding, we are passing the values of the Subject, body (content), and From address dynamically via code. It's also possible to change the values and personalize based on the needs. Note that the email will be sent to the end user who got registered by providing an email address.

4. Let's run a test by adding a new input field email to the test request payload, shown as follows:

```
{
    "firstname": "Praveen",
    "lastname": "Sreeram",
    "email":"example@gmail.com",
    "ProfilePicUrl":"A Valid url here"
}
```

5. This is the screenshot of the email that I have received:

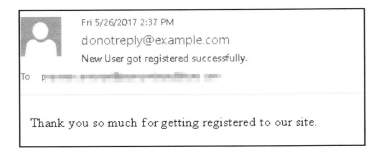

How it works...

We have updated the code of the RegisterUser function to accept another new parameter named email.

The function accepts the email parameter and sends the email to the end user using the SendGrid API. We have also configured all the other parameters, such as the From address, Subject, and body (content) in the code so that it is customized dynamically based on the requirements. We can also clear the fields in the **SendGrid output (message)** bindings, as shown in the following screenshot:

The values specified in the code will take precedence over the values specified in the preceding step.

There's more...

You can also send HTML content in the body to make your email more attractive. The following is a simple example, where I just applied bold (<b>) tag to the name of the end user:

```
message.From = new Email("donotreply@example.com");
message.AddContent(new Content("text/html","Thank you <b>" + firstname + "
" + lastname +"</b> so much for getting registered to our site."));

Personalization personalization = new Personalization();
```

The following is the screenshot of the email with my name in bold:

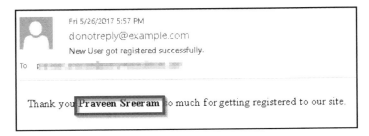

See also

- The *Sending an email notification to the administrator of the website using the SendGrid service* recipe in `Chapter 2`, *Working with Notifications Using SendGrid and Twilio Services*

Implementing email logging in the Blob storage

In most of the applications, you would have requirements of sending emails in the form of notifications, alerts, and so on to the end user. At times, users might complain that they haven't received any email even though we don't see any error in the application while sending such notification alerts.

There might be multiple reasons why users might not have received the email. Each of the email service providers has different spam filters that might block the emails in sending them to the end user's inbox. These emails might have some important information that the users might need. It makes sense to store the email content of all the emails that are sent to the end users, which could be used for retrieving the data at a later stage or for troubleshooting any unforeseen issues.

You will learn how to create a new email log file with the `.log` extension for each new registration. This log file could be used as a redundancy to the data stored in the Table storage.

In this recipe, you will learn how to store the email log files as a Blob in a storage container with the data inputted by the end user while getting registered.

How to do it...

1. Navigate to the **Integrate** tab of the `RegisterUser` function, click on **New Output** , and choose **Azure Blob Storage**.
2. Provide the required parameters in the **Azure Blob Storage output (outputBlob)** section, as shown in the following screenshot. Note the `.log` extension in the **Path** field:

3. Navigate to the code editor of the `run.csx` file and make the following change:
   1. Add a new parameter `outputBlob` of type `TextWriter` to the `Run` method.
   2. Add a new string variable named `emailContent`. This variable is used to frame the content of the email. We will also use the same variable to create the log file content that is finally stored in the blob.
   3. Frame the email content by appending the required static text and the input parameters received in **Request body**:

```
public static void Run(HttpRequestMessage req,
 TraceWriter log,
 CloudTable objUserProfileTable,
 out string objUserProfileQueueItem,
 out Mail message,
 TextWriter outputBlob
)
....
....
string email = inputJson.email;
string profilePicUrl = inputJson.ProfilePicUrl;
string emailContent ;
....
....
```

```
emailContent = "Thank you <b>" + firstname + " " +
lastname +"</b> for your registration.<br><br>" +
"Below are the details that you have provided us<br>
<br>"+ "<b>First name:</b> " + firstname + "<br>" +
"<b>Last name:</b> " + lastname + "<br>" +
"<b>Email Address:</b> " + email + "<br>" +
"<b>Profile Url:</b> " + profilePicUrl + "<br><br>
<br>" + "Best Regards," + "<br>" + "Website Team";
message.AddContent(new
Content("text/html",emailContent));
....
....
outputBlob.WriteLine(emailContent);
```

4. Run a test using the same request payload that we have used in the previous recipe.
5. After running the test, the log file got created in the container named `userregistrationemaillog`:

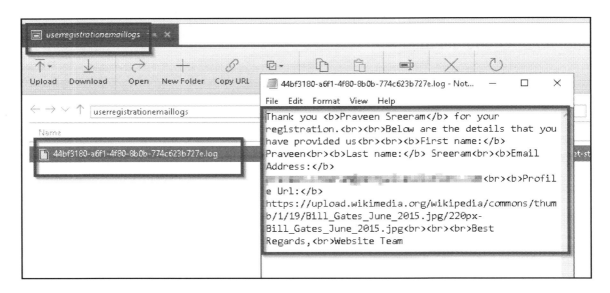

How it works...

We have created new Azure Blob output bindings. As soon as a new request is received, the email content is created and written to a new `.log` file (you can have any other extension) that is stored as a Blob in the container specified in the **Path** field of the output bindings.

Modifying the email content to include an attachment

In this recipe, you will learn how to send a file as an attachment to the registered user. In our previous recipe, we created a log file of the email content. We will send the same file as an attachment to the email. However, in real-world applications, you might not intend to send log files to the end user. For the sake of simplicity, we will send the log file as an attachment.

 At the time of writing this, SendGrid recommends that the size of the attachment not exceed 10 MB, though technically, you can have the size of your email as 30 MB.

Getting ready

This is the continuation of the previous recipe. Go through the previous recipes of this chapter just in case you are reading this first.

How to do it...

- Make the changes to the code to create the log file with the RowKey of the table. We will be achieving this using the IBinder interface.
- Send this file as an attachment to the email.

Customizing the log file name using IBinder interface

1. Navigate to the code editor of the RegisterUser function.
2. Remove the TextWriter object and replace it with the variable binder of type IBinder. This is the new signature of the Run method with the changes highlighted:

```
public static void Run(HttpRequestMessage req,
                    TraceWriter log,
                    CloudTable objUserProfileTable,
                    out string objUserProfileQueueItem,
                    out Mail message,
```

```
IBinder binder,
out SMSMessage objsmsmessage
)
```

3. Let's grab the data of the new record that's inserted into the Azure Table storage service. We will be using the GUID (RowKey) of the newly created record in the Table storage. Make the changes highlighted in the following piece of code:

```
TableResult objTableResult =
  objUserProfileTable.Execute(objTblOperationInsert);
UserProfile objInsertedUser =
(UserProfile)objTableResult.Result;
```

4. As we have removed the `TextWriter` object, the line of code `outputBlob.WriteLine(emailContent);` will no longer work. Let's replace it with the following piece of code:

```
using (var emailLogBloboutput = binder.Bind<TextWriter>(new
 BlobAttribute($"userregistrationemaillogs/
 {objInsertedUser.RowKey}.log")))
{
   emailLogBloboutput.WriteLine(emailContent);
}
```

4. Let's run a test using the same request payload that we have used in the previous recipes.

5. You will see the email log file that is created using the RowKey of the new record stored in the Azure Table storage, as shown in the following screenshot:

Adding an attachment to the email

1. Add the following code to the `Run` method of the `RegisterUser` function:

```
Attachment objAttachment = new Attachment();
objAttachment.Content = System.Convert.ToBase64String
  (System.Text.Encoding.UTF8.GetBytes(emailContent));
objAttachment.Filename = firstname + "_" + lastname + ".log";
message.AddAttachment(objAttachment);
```

2. Let's run a test using the same request payload that we have used in the previous recipes.

3. This is the screenshot of the email, along with the attachment:

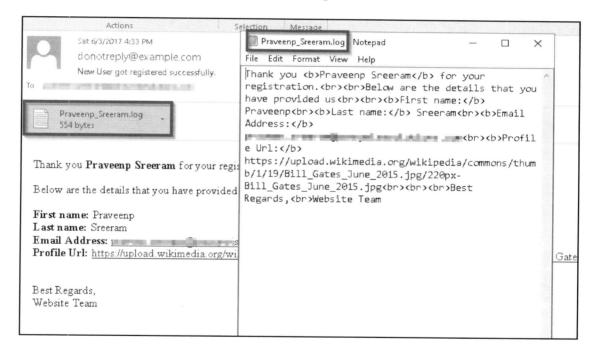

There's more...

Actions are not available for all type of output bindings. They're available only for a few, such as Blob, Queue output bindings, and so on.

Sending SMS notification to the end user using the Twilio service

In most of the previous recipes of this chapter, we have worked with SendGrid triggers to send the emails in different scenarios. In this recipe, you will learn how to send notifications via SMS using one of the leading cloud communication platform named Twilio.

> You can also learn more about Twilio at `https://www.twilio.com/`.

Getting ready

In order to use the **Twilio SMS output (objsmsmessage)** binding, we need to do the following:

1. Create a trail Twilio account from `https://www.twilio.com/try-twilio`.
2. After successful creation of the account, grab **ACCOUNT SID** and **AUTH TOKEN** from the Twilio **Dashboard**, as shown in the following screenshot. We will create two **App settings** in the **Application settings** blade of the function app for both of these settings:

3. In order to start sending messages, you need to create an active number within Twilio, which you can use as the *from number* that you could use for sending the SMS. You can create and manage numbers in **Phone Numbers Dashboard**. Navigate to `https://www.twilio.com/console/phone-numbers/incoming` and click on the **Get Started** button, as shown in the following screenshot:

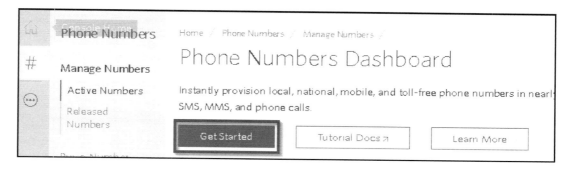

4. On the **Get Started with Phone Numbers** page, click on **Get your first Twilio phone number**, as shown in the following screenshot:

5. Once you get your number, it will be listed as follows:

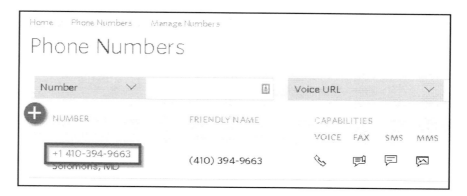

6. The final step is to verify a number to which you would like to send an SMS. You can have only one number in your trail account. You can verify a number on the `https://www.twilio.com/console/phone-numbers/verified` page. The following is the screenshot of the list of verified numbers:

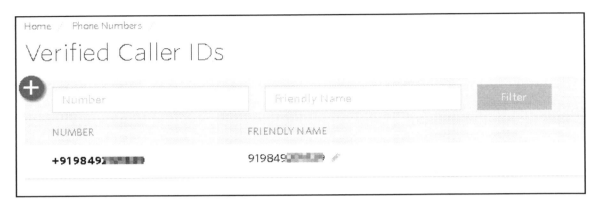

How to do it...

1. Navigate to the **Application settings** blade of the function app and add two keys to store **TwilioAccountSID** and **TwilioAuthToken,** as shown here:

2. Go the **Integrate** tab of the `RegisterUser` function and click on **New Output** and choose **Twilio SMS**, as shown in the following screenshot:

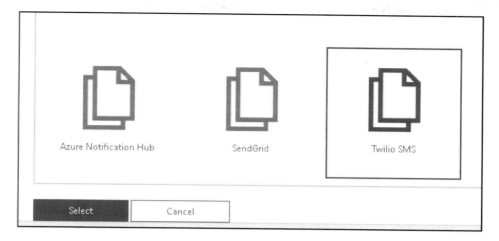

3. Click on **Select** and provide the following values to the **Twilio SMS output (objsmsmessage)** bindings. **From number** is the one that is generated in the Twilio portal, which we discussed in the *Getting Ready* section of this recipe:

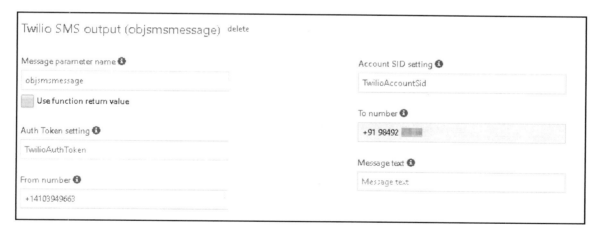

4. Navigate to the code editor and add the following lines of code, highlighted in bold. In the preceding code, I have hard coded **To number**. However, in real-world scenarios, you would dynamically receive the end user's mobile number and send the SMS via code:

```
...
...
#r "Twilio.Api"
...
...
```

```
using Twilio;
public static void Run(HttpRequestMessage req,
                        TraceWriter log,
                        CloudTable objUserProfileTable,
                        out string objUserProfileQueueItem,
                        out Mail message,
                        TextWriter outputBlob,
                        out SMSMessage objsmsmessage
                        )
    message.AddAttachment(objAttachment);
    objsmsmessage= new SMSMessage();
    objsmsmessage.Body = "Hello.. Thank you for getting
      registered.";
```

5. I just did a test run of the `RegisterUser` function using the request payload, shown as follows:

```
{
    "firstname": "Praveen",
    "lastname": "Sreeram",
    "email":"example@gmail.com",
    "ProfilePicUrl":"A Valid url here"
}
```

6. The following is the screenshot of the SMS that I have received:

How it works...

We have created a new Twilio account and copied the account ID and App key into the **App settings** of the Azure Function app. These two settings will be used by the function app runtime to connect to the Twilio API for sending the SMS.

For the sake of simplicity, I have hardcoded the phone number in the output bindings. However, in real-work applications, you would send the SMS to the phone number provided by the end users.

3
Seamless Integration of Azure Functions with Other Azure Services

In this chapter, we will cover the following recipes:

- Using Cognitive Services to locate faces from the images
- Azure SQL Database interactions using Azure Functions
- Processing a file stored in OneDrive using an external file trigger
- Monitoring tweets using Logic Apps and notifying when popular user tweets
- Integrating Logic Apps with Serverless functions

Introduction

One of the major goals of Azure Functions is to make the developers focus on just developing the application requirements and logic and abstract everything else.

As a developer or business user, you cannot afford to invent and develop your own applications from scratch for each of your business needs. You would first need to research about the existing systems and see if they fit for your business requirement. Many times, it would not be easy to understand the APIs of the other systems and integrate them as someone else has developed those APIs.

Azure provides many connectors that you could leverage to integrate your business applications with other systems pretty easily.

In this chapter we will learn how easy is to integrate different services that are available in Azure ecosystem.

Using Cognitive Services to locate faces from the images

In this recipe, you will learn how to use the Computer Vision API to detect faces within an image. We will be locating the faces and capture their coordinates and save them in different Azure Table Storage based on the gender.

Getting ready

To get started, we need to create a Computer Vision API and configure the keys to access the API in the Azure Function app.

Make sure that you have Azure Storage Explorer installed and have also configured to access the storage where you are uploading the Blobs.

Creating a new Computer Vision API account

1. Log in to Azure Management portal. Click on the + icon, choose **AI + Cognitive Services**, and choose **Computer Vision API**, as shown in the following screenshot:

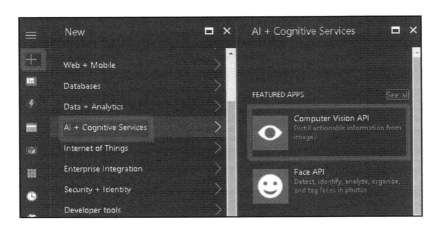

2. The next step is to provide all the details to create an account, as shown in the following screenshot. At the time of writing this, **Computer Vision API** has just two pricing tiers where I have selected the free one F0, which allows 20 API calls per minute and is limited to 5k calls each month:

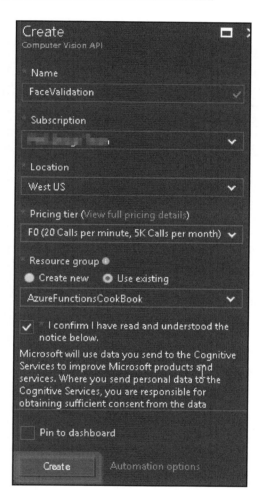

Configuring App settings

1. Once the Computer Vision API account is generated, you can navigate to the **Keys** blade and grab any of the following keys, as shown in the following screenshot:

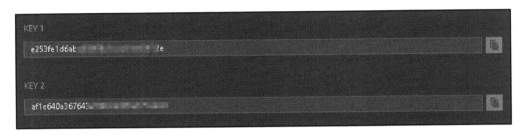

2. Navigate to your Azure Function app, create **Application settings** with the name `Vision_API_Subscription_Key`, and use any of the preceding keys as the value for the new **App settings**. This key will be used by the Azure Functions Runtime to connect and consume the Computer Vision Cognitive Service API.

How to do it...

1. Create a new function using one of the default templates named **FaceLocator-CSharp**. You can refine the templates by choosing **C#** in the **Language** drop-down and **Samples** in the **Scenario** drop-down:

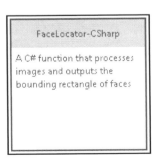

2. Once you choose the template, you need to provide the name of the Azure Function along with the **Path** and **Storage account connection**. We will upload a picture to **Azure Blob Storage trigger (image)** container (mentioned in the **Path** parameter in the following screenshot) at the end of this section:

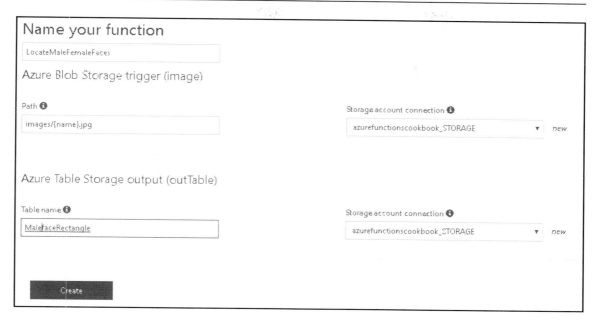

Note that while creating the function, the template creates one **Blob Storage Table output** binding and allows us to provide the name of the **Table name** parameter. However, we cannot assign the name of the parameter while creating the function. We will be able to change it after it is created. Once you have reviewed all the details, click on the **Create** button to create the Azure Function.

3. Once the function is created, navigate to the **Integrate** tab and rename the **Table parameter name** of the output binding to outMaleTable then click on the **Save** button, as shown in the following screenshot:

4. Let's create another **Azure Table Storage output** binding to store all the information for women by clicking on the **New Output** button in the **Integrate** tab, selecting **Azure Table Storage**, and clicking on the **Select** button. This is how it looks after providing the input values:

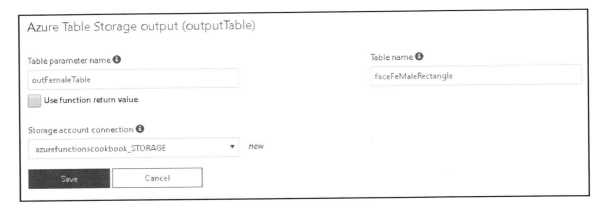

5. Once you have reviewed all the details, click on the **Save** button to create the **Azure Table Storage output** binding to store the details about women.

6. Navigate to the code editor of the Run method and add the outMaleTable and outFemaleTable parameters. This is how it should look:

```
public static async Task Run(Stream image, string name,
    IAsyncCollector<FaceRectangle> outTable,
    IAsyncCollector<FaceRectangle> outMaleTable,
    IAsyncCollector<FaceRectangle> outFemaleTable,
    TraceWriter log)
```

7. Let's add a condition (highlighted in **bold** in the following code) to check the gender and based on the gender, store the information in the respective Table storage:

```
foreach (Face face in imageData.Faces)
{
    var faceRectangle = face.FaceRectangle;
    faceRectangle.RowKey = Guid.NewGuid().ToString();
    faceRectangle.PartitionKey = "Functions";
    faceRectangle.ImageFile = name + ".jpg";
    if(face.Gender=="Female")
    {
        await outFemaleTable.AddAsync(faceRectangle);
    }
    else
```

```
{
    await outMaleTable.AddAsync(faceRectangle);
}
}
```

8. Let's upload a picture with a male and a female to the container named `images` using Azure Storage Explorer.

9. The function gets triggered as soon as I upload an image. This is the JSON that was logged in the log console of the function:

```
{
    "requestId":"483566bc-7d4d-45c1-87e2-6f894aaa4c29",
    "metadata":{   },
    "faces":[
    {
        "age":31,
        "gender":"Female",
        "faceRectangle":{
         "left":535,
         "top":182,
         "width":165,
         "height":165
        }
    },
    {
        "age":33,
        "gender":"Male",
        "faceRectangle":{
        "left":373,
        "top":182,
        "width":161,
        "height":161
        }
    }
    ]
}
```

 If you are a frontend developer with expertise in HTML5- and canvas-related technologies, you can even draw squares, which locates the faces in the image using the information provided by the cognitive services.

10. The function has also created two different Azure Table Storage tables, as shown here:

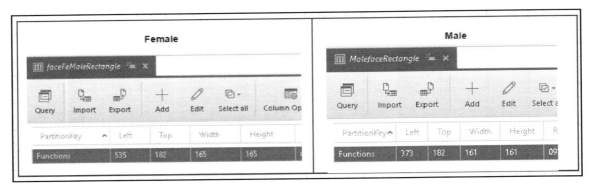

How it works...

Initially, while creating the Azure Function using the face locator template, it creates a Table storage output binding. We have used it to store the details about all the men. Later, we created another output Table storage output binding to store the details about all the women.

While we use all the default code that Azure Function templates provides to store all the face coordinates in a single table, we just made a small change that checks whether the person in the photo is male or female and stores the data based on the gender of the person identified.

 Note that the APIs don't guarantee you that they will always provide the right gender. So, in your production environments, you should have a fallback mechanism to handle such situations.

There's more...

 `ICollector` and `IAsyncCollector` are used for the bulk insertion of the data.

The default code that the template provides invokes the Computer Vision API by passing the image that we have uploaded to the Blob storage. The face locator templates invoke the API call by passing the `visualFeatures=Faces` parameter, which returns information about the following:

- Age
- Gender
- Coordinates of the faces in the picture

 You can learn more about the Computer Vision API at `https://docs.microsoft.com/en-in/azure/cognitive-services/computer-vision/home`.

Use the `Environment.GetEnvironmentVariable("KeyName")` function to retrieve the information stored in the **App settings**. In this case, the `CallVisionAPI` method uses the function to retrieve the key that is essential for making a request to the Microsoft Cognitive Services.

 It's a best practice to store all the keys and other sensitive information in **App settings** of the function app.

Azure SQL Database interactions using Azure Functions

So far, you have learned how to store data in Azure Storage services such as Blobs, Queues, and Tables. All these storage services are great for storing non-structured or semi-structured data. However, we might have requirements for storing data in relational database management systems such as Azure SQL Database.

In this recipe, you will learn how to utilize ADO.NET API to connect to the Azure SQL Database and insert JSON data into a table named `EmployeeInfo`.

Getting ready

Navigate to the Azure Management portal and create the following:

1. Create a logical SQL Server named `AzureCookbook` in the same resource group where you have your Azure Functions.

2. Create an Azure SQL Database named `Cookbookdatabase` by choosing **Blank Database** in the **Select Source** drop-down of the **SQL Database** blade while creating the database.

3. Create a firewall rule to your IP address so that you can connect to the Azure SQL Databases using **SQL Server Management Studio** (**SSMS**). If you don't have SSMS, install the latest version of SSMS. You can download it from `https://docs.microsoft.com/en-us/sql/ssms/download-sql-server-management-studio-ssms`.

4. Click on the **Show database connection strings** link in the **Essentials** blade of SQL Database, as shown in the following screenshot:

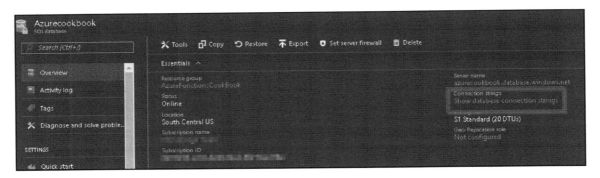

5. Copy the connection string from the following blade. Make sure that you replace the `your_username` and `your_password` templates with your actual username and password:

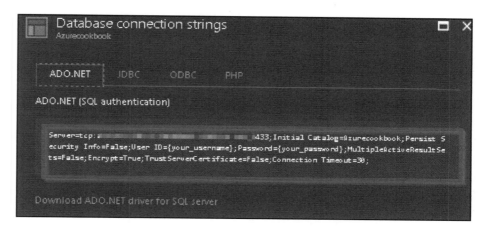

6. Open your SSMS and connect to the Azure logical SQL Server that you created in the previous steps.

7. Once you connect, create a new table named `EmployeeInfo` using the following schema:

```
CREATE TABLE [dbo].[EmployeeInfo](
[PKEmployeeId] [bigint] IDENTITY(1,1) NOT NULL,
[firstname] [varchar](50) NOT NULL,
[lastname] [varchar](50) NULL,
[email] [varchar](50) NOT NULL,
[devicelist] [varchar](max) NULL,
CONSTRAINT [PK_EmployeeInfo] PRIMARY KEY CLUSTERED
(
 [PKEmployeeId] ASC
)
)
```

How to do it...

1. Navigate to your function app and create a new HTTP trigger using the **HttpTrigger-CSharp** template and choose **Authorization Level** as **Anonymous**, as shown in the following screenshot:

2. Navigate to the **Application settings** of the function app, as shown in the following screenshot:

3. In the **Application settings** blade, under the **Connection strings** section, create a new connection string by providing the following values:
   - **Name of the Connection String**: An identifier of the connection string
   - **Value of the Connection String**: Paste the connection string that you have copied from the **Show database connection strings** section
   - **Database Type**: Select **SQL Database**

4. Navigate to the code editor of `run.csx` and replace the default code with the following:

```
#r "System.Data"
#r "System.Configuration"
using System.Net;
using System.Data.SqlClient;
using System.Data;
using System.Configuration;
public static async Task<HttpResponseMessage>
 Run(HttpRequestMessage req, TraceWriter log)
{
    dynamic data = await req.Content.ReadAsAsync<object>();
    string firstname, lastname, email,  devicelist;
    firstname = data.firstname;
    lastname = data.lastname;
    email = data.email;
    devicelist = data.devicelist;
    SqlConnection con =null;
    try
    {
        string query = "INSERT INTO EmployeeInfo (firstname,
          lastname, email, devicelist) " +  "VALUES (@firstname,
          @lastname, @email, @devicelist) ";
        con = new
          SqlConnection(ConfigurationManager.ConnectionStrings
          ["MyConnectionString"].ConnectionString);
        SqlCommand cmd = new SqlCommand(query, con);
        cmd.Parameters.Add("@firstname", SqlDbType.VarChar,
          50).Value = firstname;
        cmd.Parameters.Add("@lastname", SqlDbType.VarChar, 50)
          .Value = lastname;
        cmd.Parameters.Add("@email", SqlDbType.VarChar, 50)
          .Value = email;
        cmd.Parameters.Add("@devicelist", SqlDbType.VarChar)
          .Value = devicelist;
        con.Open();
        cmd.ExecuteNonQuery();
    }
```

```
catch(Exception ex)
{
    log.Info(ex.Message);
}
finally
{
    if(con!=null)
    {
        con.Close();
    }
}
return req.CreateResponse(HttpStatusCode.OK, "Hello ");
}
```

 Note that you need to validate each and every input parameter. For the sake of simplicity, the code that validates the input parameters is not included. Make sure that you validate each and every parameter before you save it into your database.

5. Let's run the HTTP trigger using the following test data right from the **Test** console of Azure Functions:

```
{
    "firstname": "Praveen",
    "lastname": "Kumar",
    "email": "praveen@example.com",
    "devicelist":
        "[
            {
              'Type' : 'Mobile Phone',
              'Company':'Microsoft'
            },
            {
                'Type' : 'Laptop',
                'Company':'Lenovo'
            }
        ]"
}
```

6. A record was inserted successfully, as shown in the following screenshot:

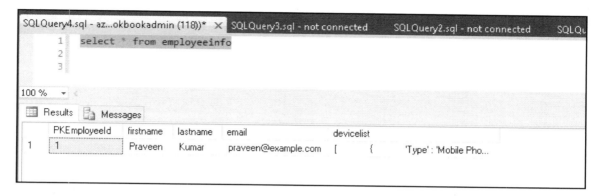

How it works...

The goal of this recipe was to accept input values from the user and save them to a relational database where the data could be retrieved later for operational purposes. For this, we used Azure SQL Database, a relational database offering also known as **database as a service (DBaaS)**. We have created a new SQL database, created firewall rules that allow us to connect remotely from the local development workstation using SSMS. We have also created a table named `EmployeeInfo`, which can be used to save the data.

We have developed a simple program using the ADO.NET API that connects to the Azure SQL Database and inserts data into the `EmployeeInfo` table.

Processing a file stored in OneDrive using an external file trigger

In the previous recipe, you learned how to process an individual request and store it in Azure SQL Database. At times, we might have to integrate our custom applications with different CRMs, which would not be exposed to other systems in general. So in these cases, people might share the CRM data via Excel sheets or JSON in some external file storage systems like OneDrive, FTP, and so on.

In this recipe, you will learn how to leverage the Azure Function Runtime and its templates to quickly integrate Azure Functions with OneDrive, retrieve the JSON file, process it, and store the data into Azure SQL Database.

 At the time of writing this, external file triggers are in an experimental state. It's not suggested to use them in production yet.

Getting ready

We will perform the following steps before moving to the *How to do it...* section:

1. Create a OneDrive account at `https://onedrive.live.com/`. We will authorize Azure Functions to use this account.
2. Create a folder named `CookBook`. We will be uploading the JSON file to this folder. As soon as a new `.json` file is uploaded, the Azure Function will be triggered.

How to do it...

1. Create a new Azure Function using the default templates **ExternalFileTrigger-CSharp**, as shown in the following screenshot:

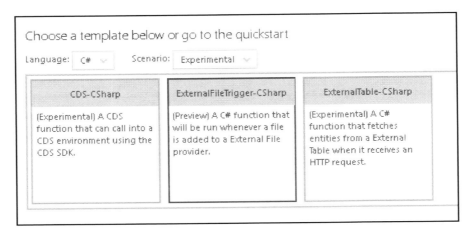

2. Provide a meaningful name and enter a valid path that you have created in your OneDrive account, as shown in the following screenshot:

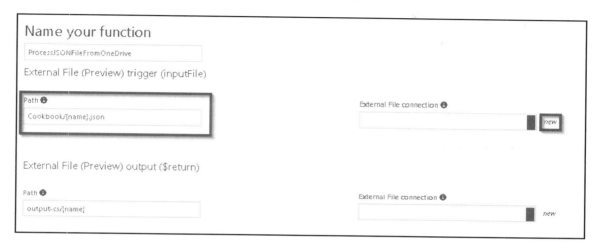

3. Click on the **new** button highlighted in the preceding screenshot to authorize access to the Azure Function Runtime from your OneDrive.

4. In **Add external file connection**, choose **OneDrive** in the **API** drop-down, and click on the **Configure required settings** button to link **External Connections**:

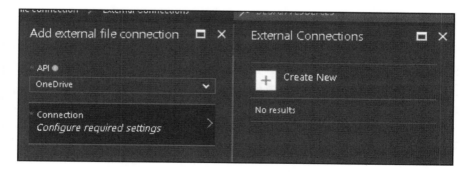

5. As you don't have any existing connections, you need to click on the **Create New** button of the preceding step, which would take you through a set of operations that prompts you to enter your OneDrive account and click on the **Authorize** button. Clicking on the **Authorize** button lets Azure Functions access your OneDrive account. Repeat the same steps for the **External File (Preview) output ($return)** section's **External File connection** drop-down, as shown in the following screenshot, and click on the **Create** button to create the Azure Function. Let the value of the **Path** be as it is. We will not need the **External File (Preview) output ($return)** binding. We will delete it in a moment:

6. Once you are ready, click on the **Create** button to create the Azure Function.
7. Once the Azure Function is created, navigate to the **Integrate** tab, click on the **External File (Preview) ($return)** output binding, as shown in the following screenshot:

8. The **ExternalFileTrigger-CSharp** Azure Function template creates a default output binding. We don't need it for our example. Let's delete the output bindings by clicking on the **delete** button highlighted in the following screenshot:

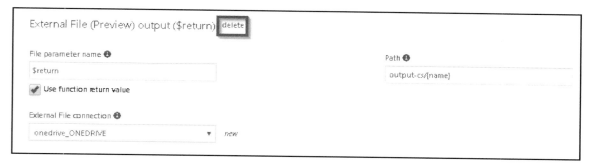

9. Navigate to the code editor of the run.csx file and replace the default code with the following code then click on the **Save** button. In this code sample, we are just outputting the elements of the JSON file that we uploaded to the OneDrive. In real-time scenarios, you might have to save them to a persistent medium, such as database that is not demonstrated in this example:

```csharp
#r "Newtonsoft.Json"
using Newtonsoft.Json;
using System;
public static void Run(string inputFile, string name,
  TraceWriter log)
{
    log.Info($"C# External trigger function processed file: " +
    name);
    var jsonResults = JsonConvert.DeserializeObject<dynamic>
    (inputFile);
    for(int nIndex=0;nIndex<jsonResults.Count;nIndex++)
    {
       log.Info(Convert.ToString(jsonResults[nIndex].firstname
       ));
       log.Info(Convert.ToString(jsonResults[nIndex].firstname
       ));
       log.Info(Convert.ToString(jsonResults[nIndex].devicelist
       ));
    }
}
```

10. Let's create a JSON file that has all the data related to the employee contact information and the details of the devices that he/she possesses. This is the structure of the JSON content:

```json
{
    "firstname": "Srikaracharya",
    "lastname": "Vatkanambi",
    "email": "vsrikar@gmail.com",
    "devicelist":
    [
        {   "DeviceType": "iPhone",
            "Color":"White"
        },
        {   "DeviceType": "Laptop",
            "Color":"Black"
        }
    ]
}
```

11. I have created a sample `.json` file with three test records and uploaded them to my OneDrive account, as shown in the following screenshot:

12. As soon as the file is uploaded to the OneDrive, the function gets triggered and prints the contents of the file in the Azure Function **Logs**, as shown in the following screenshot:

```
Logs

2017-06-10T13:39:41.695 C# External trigger function processed file: EmployeeInfo
2017-06-10T13:39:41.726 Srikaracharya
2017-06-10T13:39:41.726 Vatkanambi
2017-06-10T13:39:41.741 [
  {
    "DeviceType": "iPhone",
    "Color": "White"
  },
  {
    "DeviceType": "Laptop",
    "Color": "Black"
  }
]
2017-06-10T13:39:41.741 Anil
2017-06-10T13:39:41.741 Nammi
2017-06-10T13:39:41.741 [
  {
    "DeviceType": "SmartPhone",
    "Color": "White"
  },
  {
    "DeviceType": "Laptop",
    "Color": "Red"
  }
]
2017-06-10T13:39:41.741 Manohar
2017-06-10T13:39:41.741 Yentrapragada
2017-06-10T13:39:41.741 [
  {
    "DeviceType": "BlackBerry",
```

Monitoring tweets using Logic Apps and notifying when popular users tweet

One of my colleagues who works for a social grievance management project is responsible for monitoring the problems that users post on social platforms such as Facebook, Twitter, and so on. He was facing the problem of continuously monitoring the tweets posted on his customer's Twitter handle with specific hashtags. His major job was to respond quickly to the tweets by users with a huge follower count, say, users with more than 50K followers. So, he was looking for a solution that keeps monitoring a particular hashtag and alerts him whenever an user with more than 50K followers tweets so that he can quickly have his team respond to that user.

 Note that for the sake of simplicity, we will have the condition to check for 200 followers instead of 50K followers.

Before I knew about Azure Logic Apps, I thought it would take a few weeks to learn, develop, test, and deploy such a solution. Obviously, it would take a good amount of time to learn, understand, and consume Twitter (or any other social channel) API to get the required information and build an end-to-end solution that solves the problem.

Fortunately, after learning about Logic Apps and its out-of-the-box connectors, it hardly takes 10 minutes to design a solution for the problem that my friend has described.

In this recipe, you will learn how to design a logic app that integrates with Twitter (for monitoring tweets) and Gmail (for sending emails).

Getting ready

We need to have the following to work with this recipe:

- A valid Twitter account
- A valid Gmail account

While working with the recipe, we will need to authorize Azure Logic Apps to access your accounts.

How to do it...

We will go through the following steps:

1. Create a new Logic App.
2. Design the Logic app with Twitter and Gmail connectors.
3. Test the Logic App by tweeting the tweets with the specific hashtag.

Create a new Logic App

1. Log in to the **Azure Management portal**, click on **New**, choose **Web + Mobile**, and select **Logic App**, as shown in the following screenshot:

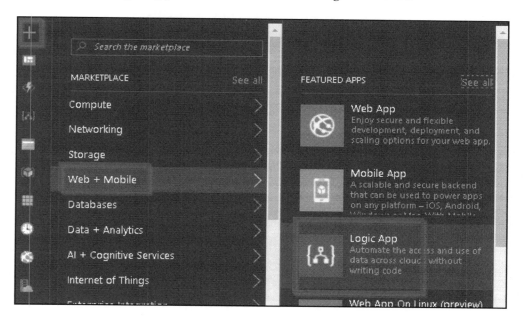

2. In the **Create logic app** blade, once you provide the **Name** of the Logic App, **Resource group**, **Subscription**, and **Location**, click on the **Create** button to create the Logic App:

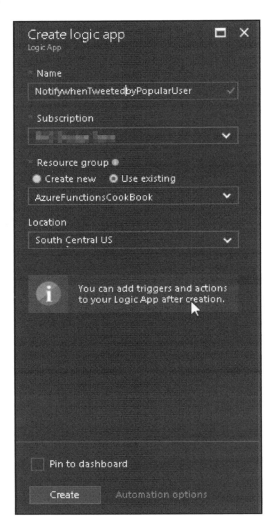

Designing the Logic App with Twitter and Gmail connectors

1. Once created, navigate to the **Logic App Designer** and choose **Blank Logic App**, as shown in the following screenshot:

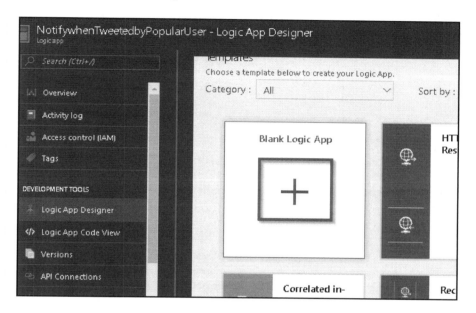

2. As soon as you choose **Blank Logic App**, you will be prompted to choose **Connectors**, as shown in the following screenshot:

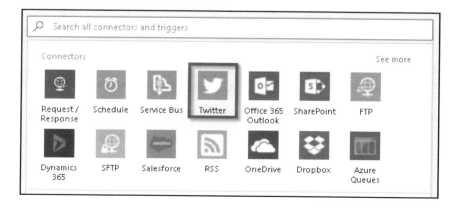

3. In the **Connectors** list, click on **Twitter**. Once you choose Twitter, you will be prompted to connect to Twitter by providing your Twitter account credentials. If you have already connected, it will directly show you the list of **Triggers** associated with the Twitter connector, as shown in the following screenshot:

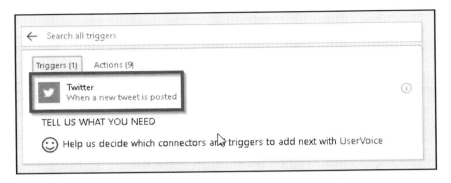

4. Once you click on the **When a new tweet is posted** trigger, you will be prompted to provide **Search text** (for example, hashtag, keywords, and so on) and the **Frequency** of which you would like the Logic App to poll the tweets. This is how it looks after you provide the details:

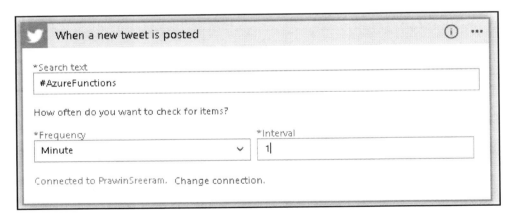

5. Let's add a new condition by clicking on **Next Step** and then clicking on **Add a condition**, as shown in the following screenshot:

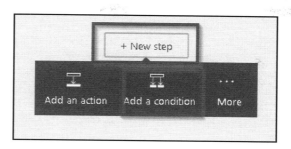

6. As soon as you click on **Add a condition**, the following screen will be displayed, where you can choose the values for the condition and choose what you would like to add when the condition evaluates to true or false:

7. When you click on the **Choose a value** input field, you will get all the parameters on which you could add a condition; in this case, we need to choose **Followers count**, as shown in the following screenshot:

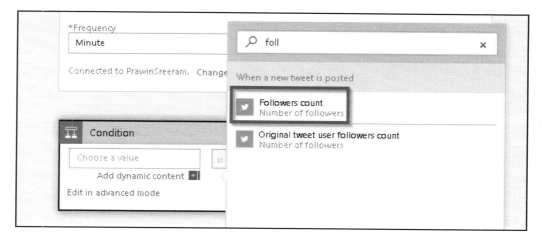

8. Once you choose the **Followers Count** parameter, you create a condition (**Followers count is greater than or equal to 200**), as shown in the following screenshot:

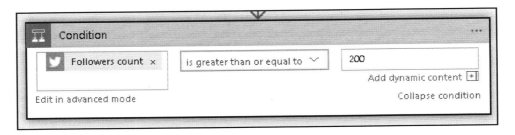

9. In the **If Yes** section of the preceding **Condition**, search for Gmail connection and select **Gmail - Send email**, as shown in the following screenshot:

10. It will ask you to log in if you haven't already. Provide your credentials and authorize Azure Logic Apps to allow access to your Gmail account.

11. Once you authorize, you can frame your email with dynamic content with the Twitter parameter, as shown in the following screenshot:

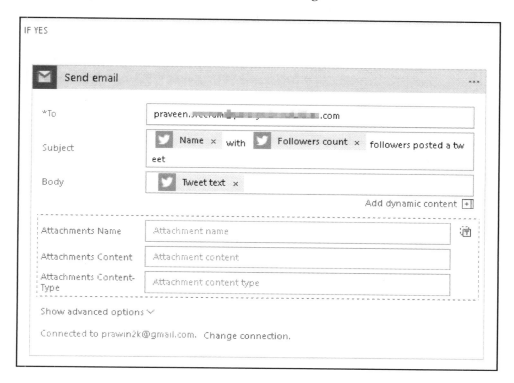

12. Once you are done, click on the **Save** button, as shown in the following screenshot:

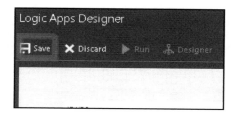

Testing the Logic App functionality

1. Let's post a tweet on Twitter with the hashtag `#AzureFunctions`, as shown in the following screenshot:

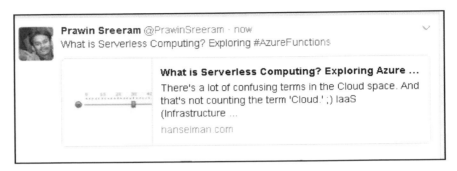

2. After a minute or so, the Logic App should have been triggered. Let's navigate to the **Overview** blade of the Logic App that we have created now and view **Runs history**:

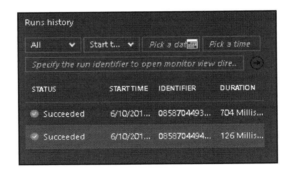

3. Yay! It has triggered twice and I have received the emails. One of them is shown in the following screenshot:

How it works...

You have created a new Logic App and have chosen the Twitter connector to monitor the tweets posted with the hashtag `#AzureFunctions` each minute. If there are any tweets with that hashtag, it checks whether the follower count ;is greater than or equal to 200. If the follower count meets the condition, then a new action is created with a new connector Gmail that is capable of sending an email with the dynamic content being framed using the Twitter connector parameters.

See also

*   The *Integrating Logic Apps with Azure Functions* recipe

Integrating Logic Apps with Azure Functions

In the previous recipe, you learned how to integrate different connectors using Logic Apps. In this recipe, we will implement the same solution that we implemented in the previous recipe by just moving the conditional logic that checks the follower count to Azure Functions.

Getting ready

Before moving further we will perform the following steps:

1. Create a SendGrid account (if not created already), grab the SendGrid API key, and create a new key in the **Application settings** of the function app.
2. Install Postman to test the **GenericWebHook-C#** trigger. You can download the tool from `https://www.getpostman.com/`.

How to do it...

1. Create a new function by choosing the **GenericWebHook-C#** trigger and name it `ValidateTwitterFollowerCount`.

2. Replace the default code with the following:

```
#r "Newtonsoft.Json"
#r "SendGrid"
using System;
using System.Net;
using Newtonsoft.Json;
using SendGrid.Helpers.Mail;
public static void Run(HttpRequestMessage req,
                       TraceWriter log,
                       out Mail message
                      )
{
    log.Info($"Webhook was triggered!");
    string jsonContent = req.Content.ReadAsStringAsync().Result;
    dynamic data = JsonConvert.DeserializeObject<dynamic>
      (jsonContent);
    string strTweet = "";
    if(data.followersCount >= 200)
    {
        strTweet = "Tweet Content" +  data.tweettext;
        message = new Mail();
        message.Subject = $"{data.Name} with
          {data.followersCount} followers has posted a tweet";
        message.From = new Email("donotreply@example.com");
        message.AddContent(new Content("text/html",strTweet));
        Personalization personalization = new Personalization();
        personalization.AddTo(new
          Email("to@gmail.com"));
        message.AddPersonalization(personalization);
    }
    else
    {
        message = null;
    }
}
```

3. Navigate to the **Integrate** tab and add a new output binding, **SendGrid**, by clicking on the **New Output** button.

4. Provide the following values in the **SendGrid output (message)** binding:

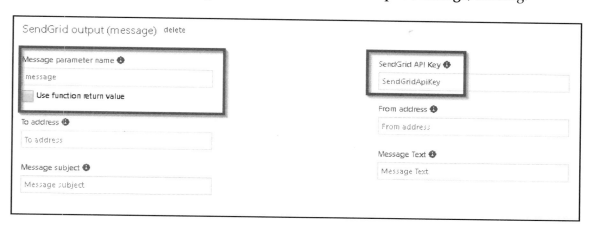

5. Test the function using Postman by choosing the parameters highlighted in the following screenshot. In the next steps, after we integrate the Azure Function `ValidateTwitterFollowerCount`, all the following input parameters, such as `followersCount`, `tweettext`, and `Name`, will be posted by the Twitter connector of the Logic App:

6. Create a new Logic App named `NotifywhenTweetedbyPopularUserUsingFunctions`.
7. Start designing the app with the **Blank Logic App** template and choose the **Twitter** connector and configure **Search text**, **Frequency**, and **Interval**.

8. Click on the **New step** to add an action by choosing the **Add an action** button, as shown in the following screenshot:

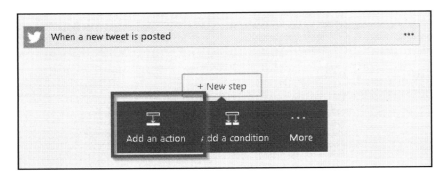

9. In the **Choose an action** section, choose **Azure Functions** as a connector, as shown in the following screenshot:

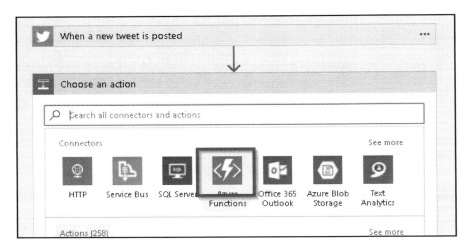

10. Clicking on **Azure Functions** shows the following action. Click on **Azure Functions - Choose an Azure function**:

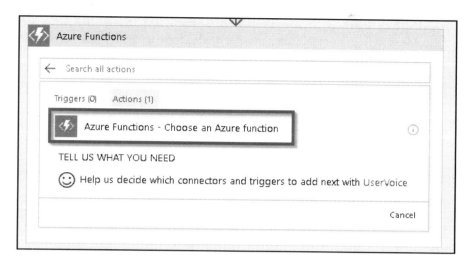

11. Now you will see all the available function apps. Click on the **AzureFunctionCookbook** function app and then select the **Azure Functions - ValidateTwitterFollowerCount** function, as shown in the following screenshot:

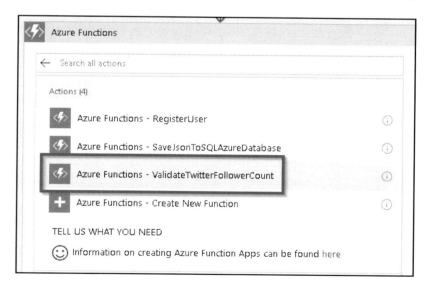

12. In the next step, you need to frame the input that needs to be passed from the Logic App to the **GenericWebHook-C#** function `ValidateTwitterFollowerCount`, which we have developed. Let's frame input JSON in the same way that we have created while testing the **GenericWebHook-C#** function using Postman, as shown in the following screenshot (the only difference is that the values such as `followersCount`, `Name`, and `tweettext` are dynamic now):

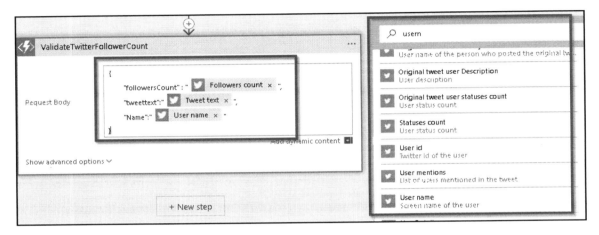

13. Once you have reviewed all the parameters that the `ValidateTwitterFollowerCount` function expects, click on the **Save** button to save the changes.
14. You can wait for a few minutes or post a tweet with the hash tag that you have configured in the **Search text** input field.

There's more...

 In the Azure Function `ValidateTwitterFollowerCount`, we have hardcoded the threshold follower count of `200` in the code. It's a good practice to store these values as configurable items by storing them in **Application settings**.

If you don't see the intended dynamic parameter, click on the **See more** button, as shown in the following screenshot:

See also

- The *Sending an email notification to the end user dynamically* recipe in `Chapter 2`, *Working with Notifications Using SendGrid and Twilio Services*

4
Understanding the Integrated Developer Experience of Visual Studio Tools for Azure Functions

In this chapter, we will cover the following :

- Creating the function app using Visual Studio 2017
- Debugging C# Azure Functions on a local staged environment using Visual Studio 2017
- Connecting to the Azure Cloud storage from local Visual Studio environment
- Deploying the Azure Function app to Azure Cloud using Visual Studio
- Debugging live C# Azure Function hosted on the Microsoft Azure Cloud environment using Visual Studio

Introduction

In all our previous chapters, we looked at how to create Azure Functions right from the Azure Management portal. The following are a few of the features:

- You can quickly create a function just by selecting one of the built-in templates provided by the Azure Function Runtime
- Developers need not worry about writing the plumbing code and understanding how the frameworks work
- Make the configuration changes right within the UI using the standard editor

In spite of all the advantages mentioned, somehow, developers might not find it comfortable as they might have become used to working with their favorite **Integrated Development Environments (IDEs)** since a long time. So, the Microsoft team has come up with some tools that help developers integrate them into the Visual Studio so that they can leverage some of the critical IDE features that accelerate the development efforts. The following are a few of them:

- You will have IntelliSense support
- You can debug the code line by line
- Quickly view the values of the variables while you are debugging the application
- Integration with version control systems such as **Visual Studio Team Services (VSTS)**

Currently, the Visual Studio tools for the function supports debugging only for C# (at the time of writing this). Microsoft would come up with all these cool features in the future for other languages. If you would prefer to use Visual Studio Code to develop Azure Functions for JavaScript (Node.js), you can have debugging support.

You will learn some of the preceding features in this chapter and see how to integrate code with VSTS in Chapter 10, *Implement Continuous Integration and Deployment of Azure Functions Using Visual Studio Team Services*.

Creating the function app using Visual Studio 2017

In this recipe, you will learn how to create an Azure Function in your favorite IDE Visual Studio 2017.

Getting ready

You need to download and install the following tools and software:

- Download Visual Studio 2017 Preview Version 15.3.0, Preview 2.0, or higher. You can download it from `https://www.visualstudio.com/vs/preview/`.
- Choose **Azure development** in the **Workloads** section while installing, as shown in the following screenshot, and click on the **Install** button.

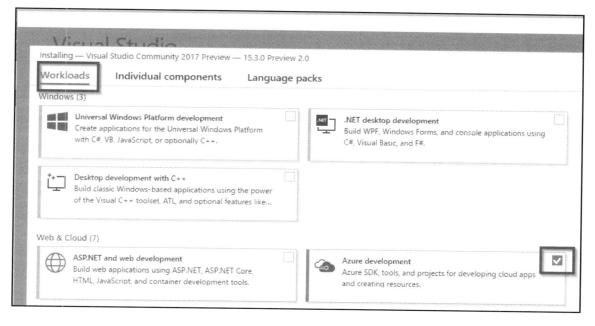

- Download Azure Function Tools for Visual Studio 2017 from `https://marketplace.visualstudio.com/items?itemName=AndrewBHall-MSFT.AzureFunctionToolsforVisualStudio2017`.

How to do it...

1. Open Visual Studio and choose **File** and then click on **New Project**. In the **New Project** dialog box, in the **Installed** templates, under **Visual C#**, select **Cloud** and then select the **Azure Functions** template:

2. Provide the name of the function app. Click on the **OK** button to create the function app after choosing a location:

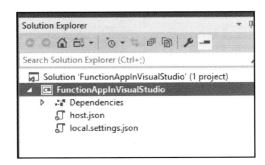

3. We have created the Azure Function successfully. Now let's add an HTTP trigger function that accepts web requests and sends a response to the client.

4. Right click on the project, click on **Add**, and select **New Item**. In the **Add New Item** window, choose **Azure Function**, as shown in the following screenshot:

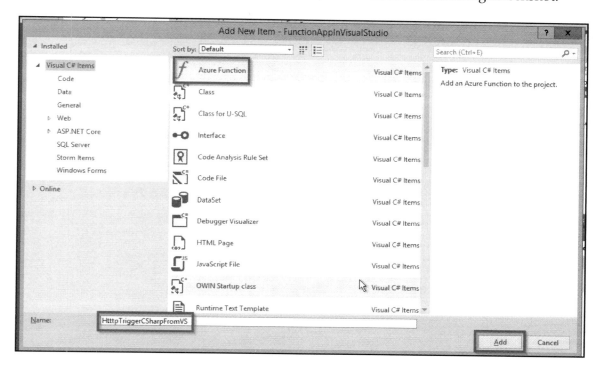

5. In the **New Azure Function** dialog box, as shown in the following screenshot, provide the required values and click on the **Create** button to create the new `HTTPTrigger` function:

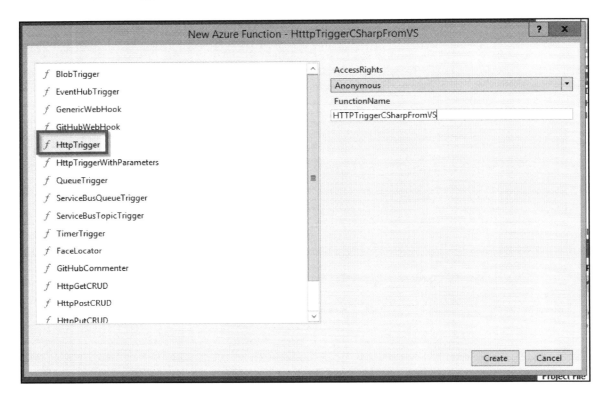

6. After you create a new function, a new class will be created, as shown in the following screenshot:

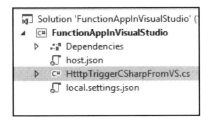

We have now successfully created a new HTTP triggered function app using our favorite IDE Visual Studio 2017.

How it works...

Visual Studio tools for Azure Functions help developers use their favorite IDE, which they have been using since ages. Using the Azure Function Tools, you can use the same set of templates that the Azure Management portal provides in order to quickly create and integrate with the cloud services without writing any (or minimal) plumbing code.

The other advantage of using Visual Studio tools for functions is that you don't need to have a live Azure subscription. You can debug and test Azure Functions right on your local development environment. Azure CLI and related utilities provide us with all the required assistance to execute the Azure Functions.

There's more...

One of the most common problems that developers face while developing any application on their local environment is that *everything works fine on my local machine but not on the production environment*. Developers need not worry about this in the case of Azure Functions. The Azure Functions Runtime provided by the Azure CLI tools is exactly the same as the runtime available on Azure Cloud.

 Note that you can always use and trigger an Azure service running on the cloud even when you are developing the Azure Functions locally.

Debugging C# Azure Functions on a local staged environment using Visual Studio 2017

Once the basic setup of creating the function is complete, the next step is to start working on developing the application as per your needs. Developing code on a daily basis is not at all a cake walk; developers will end up facing technical issues. They need tools to help them identify the root cause of the problem and fix it to make sure they are delivering the solution. These tools include debugging tools that help developers step into each line of the code and view the values of the variable and objects and get a detailed view of the exceptions.

In this recipe, you will learn how to configure and debug an Azure Function in a local development environment within Visual Studio.

Getting ready

Download and install the following:

- Azure CLI (if you don't have these tools installed, Visual Studio will automatically download them when you run your functions from Visual Studio.)

How to do it...

1. In our previous recipe, we created the `HTTPTrigger` function using Visual Studio. Let's build the application by clicking on **Build** and then clicking on **Build Solution**.
2. Open the `HTTPTriggerCSharpFromVS.cs` file and create a breakpoint by pressing the *F9* key, as shown in the following screenshot:

```
local.settings.json    HtttpTriggerCSharpFromVS.cs   + X
FunctionAppInVisualStudio                                      FunctionAppInVisualStudio.HtttpTrigg
    4      using System.Threading.Tasks;
    5      using Microsoft.Azure.WebJobs;
    6      using Microsoft.Azure.WebJobs.Extensions.Http;
    7      using Microsoft.Azure.WebJobs.Host;
    8
    9    namespace FunctionAppInVisualStudio
    10   {
    11       public static class HtttpTriggerCSharpFromVS
    12       {
    13           [FunctionName("HTTPTriggerCSharpFromVS")]
    14           public static async Task<HttpResponseMessage> Run([HttpTrigger(Authorizat
    15           {
    16               log.Info("C# HTTP trigger function processed a request.");
    17
    18               // parse query parameter
    19               string name = req.GetQueryNameValuePairs()
    20                   .FirstOrDefault(q => string.Compare(q.Key, "name", true) == 0)
    21                   .Value;
    22
```

3. Press the *F5* key to start debugging the function. When you press *F5* key for the first time, Visual Studio prompts you to download Visual Studio CLI tools. These tools are essential for executing the Azure Function in Visual Studio:

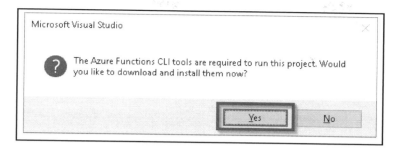

 The Azure Function CLI is now renamed to Azure Function Core Tools. You can learn more about them at `https://www.npmjs.com/package/azure-functions-core-tools`.

4. Clicking on **Yes** in the preceding step would start downloading the CLI tools. This would take a few minutes to download and install the CLI tools.

5. After the Azure Function CLI tools are installed successfully, a job host will be created and started. It starts monitoring the requests on a specific port for all the functions of our function app. The following is the screenshot that shows that the job host has started monitoring the requests to the function app:

```
C:\Users\praveen\AppData\Local\Azure.Functions.Cli\1.0.0-beta.94\func.exe        —    □    ×

Starting Host (HostId=26fd53d5e9e646d8a888e9cceb48dc97, Version=1.0.10826.0, ProcessId=7200, Debu
g=False, Attempt=0)
Executing HTTP request: {
  "requestId": "bdde0c51-f935-492d-ae97-c770c46573fa",
  "method": "GET",
  "uri": "/"
}
Executed HTTP request: {
  "requestId": "bdde0c51-f935-492d-ae97-c770c46573fa",
  "method": "GET",
  "uri": "/",
  "authorizationLevel": "Anonymous"
}
Response details: {
  "requestId": "bdde0c51-f935-492d-ae97-c770c46573fa",
  "status": "OK"
}
Found the following functions:
Host.Functions.HttpTriggerCSharpFromVS

Job host started
Http Function HttpTriggerCSharpFromVS: http://localhost:7071/api/HttpTriggerCSharpFromVS
Debugger listening on [::]:5858
```

6. Let's try to access the function app by making a request to
   `http://localhost:7071` in one of your favorite browsers:

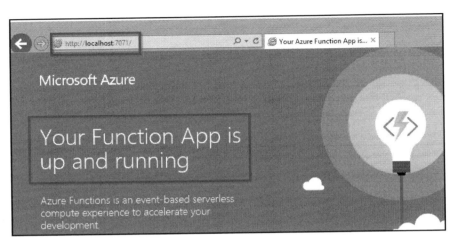

7. Now, key in the complete URL of our HTTP trigger in the browser. It should look like this:
   `http://localhost:7071/api/HttpTriggerCsharpFromVS?name=Praveen Sreeram`

8. As soon as we hit the *Enter* key in the location bar of your browser after typing the correct URL of the Azure Function, the Visual Studio debugger hits the debugging point (if you have one), as shown in the following screenshot:

```csharp
using System.Threading.Tasks;
using Microsoft.Azure.WebJobs;
using Microsoft.Azure.WebJobs.Extensions.Http;
using Microsoft.Azure.WebJobs.Host;

namespace FunctionAppInVisualStudio
{
    public static class HttptTriggerCSharpFromVS
    {
        [FunctionName("HTTPTriggerCSharpFromVS")]
        public static async Task<HttpResponseMessage> Run([HttpTrigger(Authorizat
        {
            log.Info("C# HTTP trigger function processed a request.");

            // parse query parameter
            string name = req.GetQueryNameValuePairs()
                .FirstOrDefault(q => string.Compare(q.Key, "name", true) == 0)
                .Value;
```

9. You can also view the data of your variables, as shown in the following screenshot:

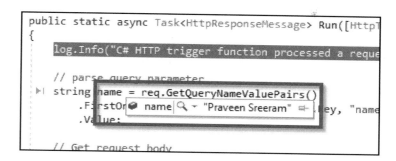

10. Once you complete the debugging, you can click on the *F5* key to complete the execution process. Once the execution of the entire function is complete, you would see the output response in the browser, as shown in the following screenshot:

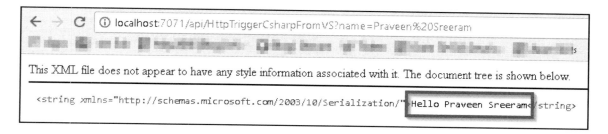

11. The function execution log will be seen in the job host console, as shown in the following screenshot:

12. You can add more Azure Functions to the function app, if required. In the next recipe, we will look at how to connect to Azure Cloud storage from the local environment.

How it works...

The job host works as a server that listens to a specific port. If there are any requests to that particular port, it automatically takes care of executing the requests and sends a response.

The job host console provides you with the following details:

- The status of the execution along with the request and response data
- The details about all the functions available in the function app

There's more...

Using Visual Studio, you can directly create precompiled functions, which means when you build your functions, it creates a `.dll` file that can be referenced in other applications, as you do for your regular classes. The following are two of the advantages of using precompiled functions:

- Precompiled functions have better performance as they wouldn't be required to compile on the fly
- You can convert your traditional classes into Azure Functions easily and refer them in other applications seamlessly

Connecting to the Azure Cloud storage from local Visual Studio environment

In both of the previous recipes, you learned how to create and execute Azure Functions in a local environment. We have triggered the function from a local browser. However, in this recipe, you will learn how to trigger an Azure Function in your local environment when an event occurs in Azure. For example, when a new Blob is created in a storage account, you can have your function triggered on your local machine. This helps the developers test their applications upfront before they deploy them to the production environment.

Getting ready

1. Create a storage account and a container named `cookbookfiles` in Azure.
2. Install Microsoft Azure Storage Explorer from `http://storageexplorer.com/`.

How to do it...

1. Open the **FunctionAppInVisualStudio** Azure Function app in Visual Studio and add a new function named `BlobTriggerCSharp`, as shown in the following screenshot:

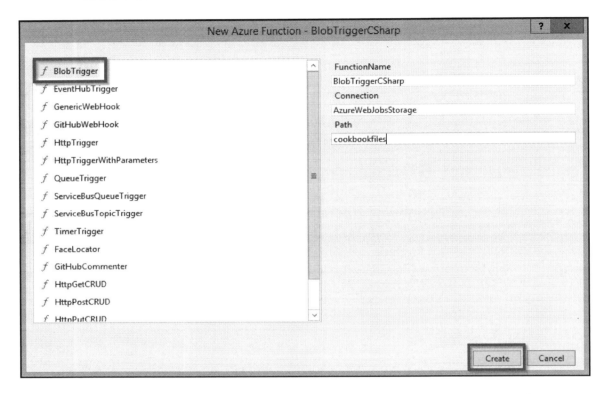

2. In the storage account connection, provide `AzureWebJobsStorage` as the name of the connection string and also provide the name of the Blob container (in my case, it is `cookbookfiles`) in the **Path** input field and click on the **Create** button to create the new Blob trigger function.

3. A new Blob trigger function gets created, as shown in the following screenshot:

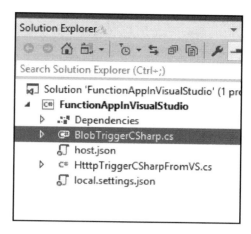

4. If you remember the *Building a backend Web API using HTTP triggers* recipe from Chapter 1, *Accelerate Your Cloud Application Development Using Azure Function Triggers and Bindings*, the Azure Management portal allowed us to choose a new or existing storage account. However, the preceding dialog box is not connected to your Azure subscription. So, you need to navigate to the storage account and copy the connection string by navigating to the **Access Keys** blade of the storage account in the Azure Management portal, as shown in the following screenshot:

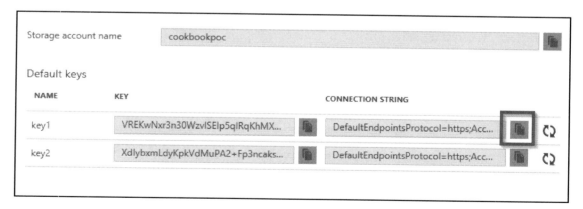

5. Once you have copied the connection string, paste it in the `local.settings.json` file, which is in the `root` folder of the project. This file is created when you create the function app. The `local.settings.json` file should look something like what is shown in the following screenshot after you add the connection string to the key named `AzureWebJobsStorage`:

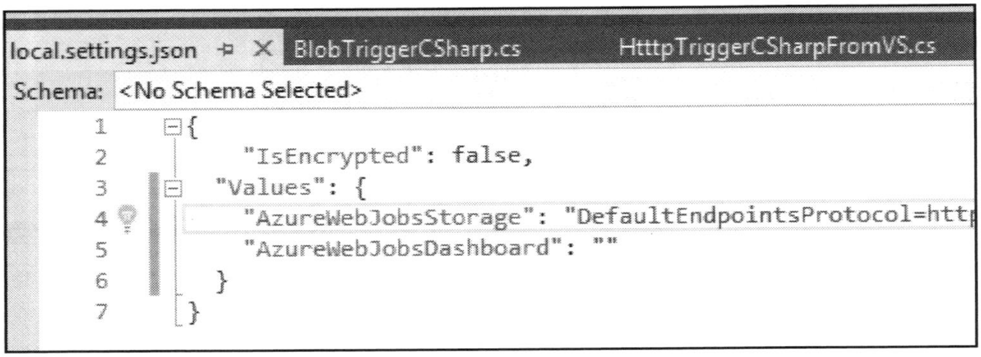

6. Open the `BlobTriggerCSharp.cs` file and create a breakpoint, as shown in the following screenshot:

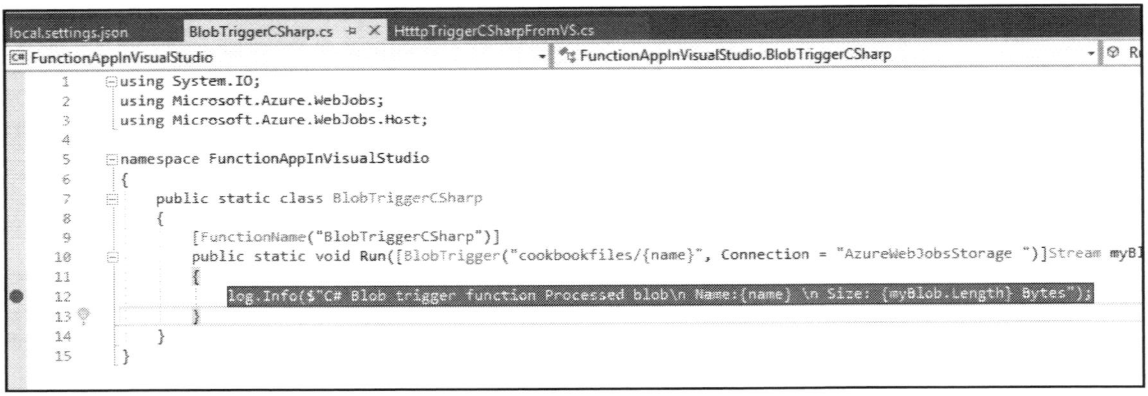

7. Now press the *F5* key to start the job host, as shown in the following screenshot:

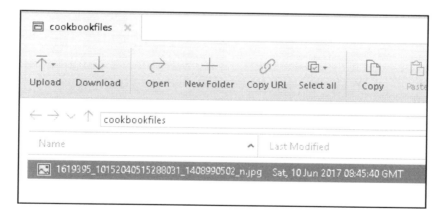

8. I have added a new Blob file using Azure Storage Explorer, as shown in the following screenshot:

9. As soon as the Blob has been added to the specified container (in this case, it is `cookbookfiles`), which is sitting in the cloud in a remote location, the job host running in my local machine detects that a new Blob has been added and the debugger hits the function, as shown in the following screenshot:

```
host.json          local.settings.json     BlobTriggerCSharp.cs  ☐ ✕  HttptTriggerCSharpFromVS.cs ☐ ✕
C# FunctionAppInVisualStudio                              ▼  ✓ FunctionAppInVisualStudio.BlobTriggerCSharp
C:\Users\Cookbookadmin\Source\Repos\Chapter4\FunctionAppInVisualStudio\FunctionAppInVisualStudio\HttptTriggerCSharpFromVS.cs
   2        using Microsoft.Azure.WebJobs;
   3        using Microsoft.Azure.WebJobs.Host;
   4
   5      ☐ namespace FunctionAppInVisualStudio
   6        {
   7      ☐     public static class BlobTriggerCSharp
   8            {
   9                [FunctionName("BlobTriggerCSharp")]
  10      ☐        public static void Run([BlobTrigger("cookbookfiles/{name}", Connection = "AzureWebJobsStorage")]Stream m
  11                {
  12                    log.Info($"C# Blob trigger function Processed blob\n Name:{name} \n Size: {myBlob.Length} Bytes");
  13                }
  14            }
```

How it works...

In this `BlobTriggerCSharp` class, the `Run` method has the WebJobs attributes that has the connection string (in this case, it is `AzureWebJobsStorage`). This instructs the runtime to refer to the Azure Storage connection string in the local settings configuration file with the key named the `AzureWebJobsStorage` connection String. When the job host starts running, it uses the connection string and keeps an eye on the storage accounts containers that we have specified. Whenever a new Blob is added/updated, it automatically triggers the Blob trigger in the current environment.

There's more...

When you create Azure Functions in the Azure Management portal, you would need to create triggers and output bindings in the **Integrate** tab of each Azure Function. However, you can just configure WebJob attributes when you are creating the function from the Visual Studio 2017 IDE.

 You can learn more about WebJob attributes at `https://docs.microsoft.com/en-us/azure/app-service-web/websites-dotnet-webjobs-sdk`.

See also

- The *Creating the function app using Visual Studio 2017* recipe

Deploying the Azure Function app to Azure Cloud using Visual Studio

So far the function app is just a regular application within Visual Studio. To deploy the function app along with its functions, we need to either create the following new resources or select existing ones to host the new function app:

- The resource group
- The App Service plan
- The Azure Function app

You can provide all these details directly from Visual Studio without opening the Azure Management portal. You will learn how to do that in this recipe.

How to do it...

1. Right click on the project and then click on the **Publish** button to open the **Publish** window.
2. In the **Publish** window, choose the **Create New** option and click on the **Publish** button, as shown in the following screenshot:

3. In the **Create App Service** window, you can choose the existing resources or click on the **New** button to choose the new **Resource Group**, the **App Service Plan**, and the **Storage Account**, as shown in the following screenshot:

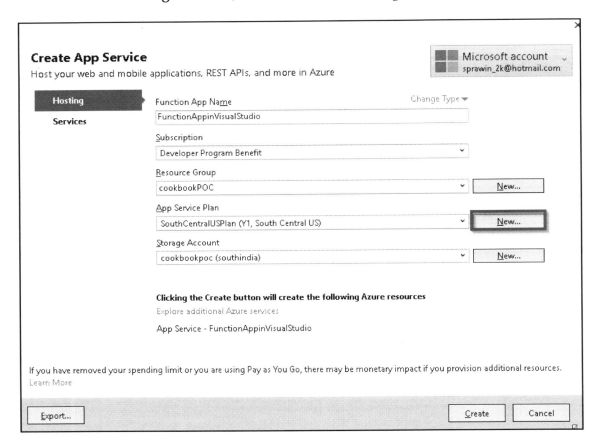

4. In most of the cases, you would like to go with **Consumption** plan for hosting the Azure Functions unless you have a strong reason and would like to utilize one of your existing App Services. To choose the **Consumption** plan, you need to click on the **New** button that is available for the App Service plan shown in the preceding screenshot. Clicking on the **New** button will open another popup, where you can choose the Consumption plan. As shown in the following screenshot, select **Consumption** in the **Size** drop-down and click on the **OK** button:

5. After reviewing all the information, click on the **Create** button of the **Create App Service** window. As soon as you click on the **Create** button, it starts deploying the services to Azure, as shown in the following screenshot:

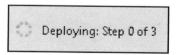

6. If everything goes fine, you can view the new function app created in the Azure Management portal, as shown in the following screenshot:

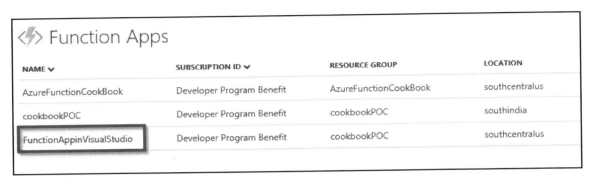

7. Hold on! Our job in Visual Studio is not yet done. We have just created the required services in Azure right from Visual Studio IDE. Our next job is to publish the code from the local workstation to Azure Cloud. As soon as the deployment is complete, you will be taken to the web deploy step, as shown in the following screenshot. Click on the **Publish** button to start the process of publishing the code to your Azure Function app:

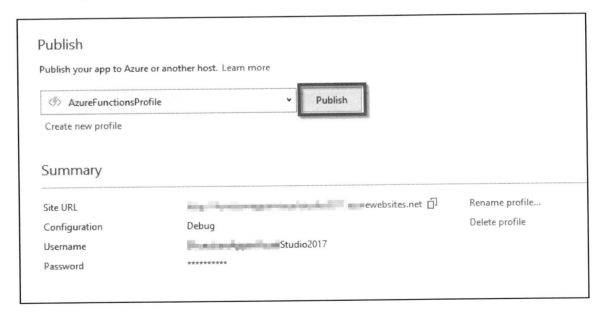

8. After a few seconds, you would see something similar in the **Output** window of your Visual Studio:

```
Output
Show output from: Build                                            ⚙ ⬚ ⬚ ⬚ ⚡ ⬚
Adding file (FunctionAppinVisualStudio\BlobTriggerCSharp\run.csx).
Adding file (FunctionAppinVisualStudio\BlobTriggerCSharp\sample.dat).
Updating file (FunctionAppinVisualStudio\host.json).
Adding file (FunctionAppinVisualStudio\HttpTriggerCSharpFromVS\function.json).
Adding file (FunctionAppinVisualStudio\HttpTriggerCSharpFromVS\project.json).
Adding file (FunctionAppinVisualStudio\HttpTriggerCSharpFromVS\project.lock.json).
Adding file (FunctionAppinVisualStudio\HttpTriggerCSharpFromVS\readme.md).
Adding file (FunctionAppinVisualStudio\HttpTriggerCSharpFromVS\run.csx).
Adding file (FunctionAppinVisualStudio\HttpTriggerCSharpFromVS\sample.dat).
Adding file (FunctionAppinVisualStudio\Project_Readme.html).
Publish Succeeded.
Web App was published successfully http://functionappinvisualstudio.azurewebsites.net/
========== Build: 1 succeeded or up-to-date, 0 failed, 0 skipped ==========
========== Publish: 1 succeeded, 0 failed, 0 skipped ==========
```

9. That's it. We have completed the deployment of your function app and its functions to Azure right from your favorite development IDE Visual Studio. You can review the function deployment in the Azure Management portal. Both Azure Functions got created successfully, as shown in the following screenshot:

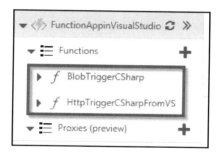

There's more...

Azure Functions that are created from Visual Studio 2017 are precompiled, which means you deploy the .dll files from Visual Studio 2017 to Azure. So, you cannot edit the functions' code in Azure after you deploy. However, you can make changes to the configurations, such as changing the Azure Storage connection string, the container path, and so on. We will look at how to do that in the next recipe.

See also

- The *Debugging live C# Azure Function hosted on the Microsoft Azure Cloud environment using Visual Studio* recipe

Debugging live C# Azure Function hosted on the Microsoft Azure Cloud environment using Visual Studio

In one of the previous recipes, in the *Connecting to the Azure Cloud storage from local Visual Studio environment* recipe, you learned how to connect the cloud storage account from the local code. In this recipe, you will learn how to debug the live code running in the Azure Cloud environment. We will be performing the following steps in the `BlobTriggerCSharp` function of the `FunctionAppinVisualStudio` function app:

- Change the path of the container in the Azure Management portal to the new container
- Open the function app in Visual Studio 2017
- Attach the debugger from within Visual Studio 2017 to the required Azure Function
- Create a Blob to the new storage container
- Debug the application after the breakpoints are hit

Getting ready

Create a container named `cookbookfiles-live` in the storage account. We will be uploading a Blob to this container.

How to do it...

1. Navigate to the `BlobTriggerCSharp` function in the Azure Management portal and change the path of the `path` variable, as shown in the following screenshot:

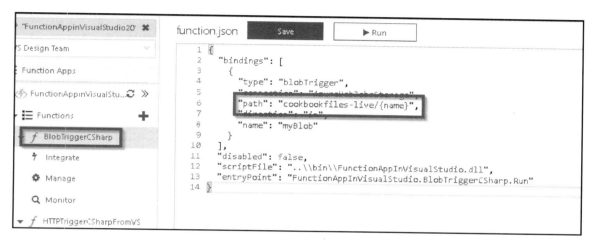

2. Open the function app in Visual Studio 2017. Open **Server Explorer** and navigate to your Azure Function, in this case, **FunctionAppinVisualStudio2017**, as shown in the following screenshot:

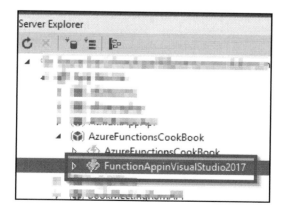

3. Right-click on the function and click on **Attach Debugger**, as shown in the following screenshot:

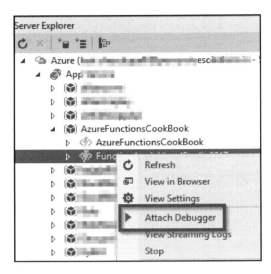

4. As soon as the **Attach Debugger** is clicked, Visual Studio will take a few moments to enable remote debugging, as shown in the following screenshot:

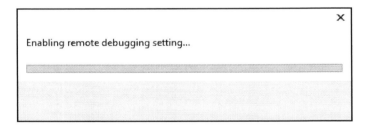

5. Once the remote debugging is enabled, the function app URL will be opened in the browser, as shown in the following screenshot, indicating that our function app is running:

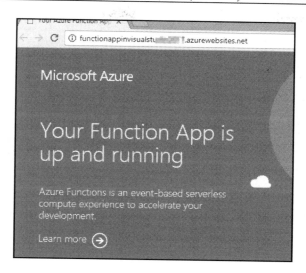

6. Navigate to **Storage Explorer** and upload a new file (in this case, I uploaded `EmployeeInfo.json`) to the `cookbookfiles-live` container, as shown in the following screenshot:

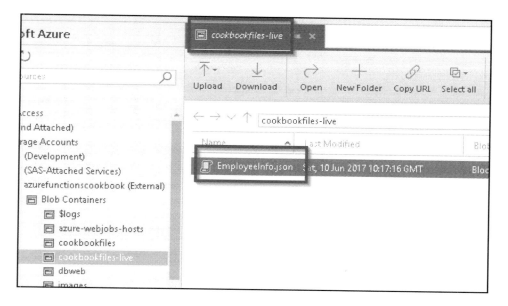

7. After a few moments, the debug breakpoint will be hit, shown as follows, where you can view the filename that has been uploaded.

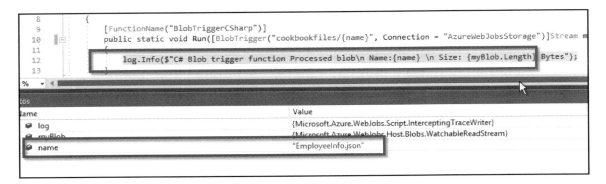

See also

- The *Connecting to the Azure Cloud storage from local Visual Studio environment* recipe

5

Exploring Testing Tools for the Validation of Azure Functions

In this chapter, we will explore different ways of testing the Azure Functions in more detail with the following recipes:

- Testing HTTP functions using the following techniques:
  - Postman
  - The Azure Management portal
  - Test Queues and Blobs using Storage Explorer
- Testing an Azure Function on a staged environment using deployment slots
- Load testing Azure Functions using **Visual Studio Team Services** (**VSTS**)
- Creating and testing Azure Function locally using Azure CLI tools
- Testing and validating Azure Function responsiveness using Application Insights

Introduction

In all our previous chapters, you learned how to develop Azure Function and where they are useful and looked at validating the functionality of those functions.

In this chapter, we will start looking at ways of testing different Azure Functions. For example, running tests of HTTP trigger functions using Postman, usage of Microsoft Storage Explorer to test Azure Blob triggers, Queue triggers, and other storage-service-related triggers. You will also learn how to perform a simple load test on an HTTP trigger to understand how the serverless architecture works on provisioning the instances in the backend without developers worrying about the scaling settings on different factors. Azure Function runtime will automatically take care of scaling the instances.

You will also learn how to set up a test that checks the availability of our functions by continuously pinging the application endpoints on a predefined frequency from multiple locations.

Testing Azure Functions

Azure Function runtime allows us to create and integrate with many Azure services. At the time of writing this, there are more than 20 types of Azure Functions you can create. You also need to understand how to test these functions. In this recipe, you will learn how to test the most common Azure Functions, listed as follows:

* Testing HTTP triggers using Postman
* Testing the Blob trigger using Microsoft Storage Explorer
* Testing the Queue trigger using the Azure Management portal

Getting ready

Install the following tools if you haven't installed them yet:

* **Postman**: You can download it from `https://www.getpostman.com/`
* **Microsoft Azure Storage Explorer**: You can download it from `http://storageexplorer.com/`

   > You can use Storage Explorer to connect to the storage accounts and view all the data available different storage services, such as Blobs, Queues, Tables, and Files. You can also create, update, and delete them right from the Storage Explorer.

How to do it...

In this section, we will create three Azure Function using the default templates available in the Azure Management portal and test them in different tools.

Testing HTTP triggers using Postman

1. Create an HTTP trigger function that accepts the First name and Last name parameters and sends them in the response. Once it is created, make sure you set **Authorization Level** as Anonymous.

2. Replace the default code with the following. Note that for the sake of simplicity, I have removed the validations. In the real-time applications, you need to validate each and every input parameter:

```
using System.Net;
public static string Run(HttpRequestMessage req, TraceWriter
 log)
{
    log.Info("C# HTTP trigger function processed a request.");
    string Firstname =
     req.GetQueryNameValuePairs().FirstOrDefault(q =>
     string.Compare(q.Key, "Firstname", true) == 0).Value;
    string Lastname =
     req.GetQueryNameValuePairs().FirstOrDefault(q =>
     string.Compare(q.Key, "Lastname", true) == 0).Value;
    return  "Hello " + Firstname + " " + Lastname;
}
```

3. Open the Postman tool and complete the following:
    1. The first step is to choose the type of HTTP method using which you would like to make the HTTP request. As our function accepts most of the methods by default, choose the **GET** method, shown as follows:

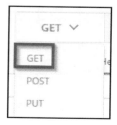

2. The next step is to provide the URL of the HTTP trigger, shown as follows:

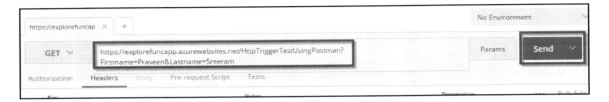

3. Click on the **Send** button to make the request. If you have provided all the details expected by the API, then you would see a **Status code = 200** along with the response.

Testing Blob trigger using the Microsoft Storage Explorer

1. Create a new Blob trigger by providing a storage account and a container where you store the Blob, shown as follows:

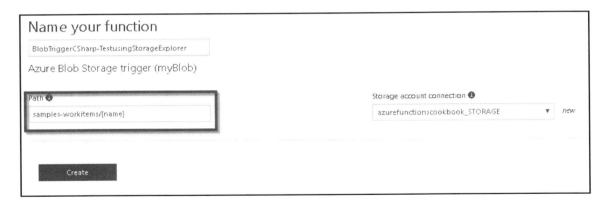

2. Let's connect to the storage account that we will be using in this recipe. Open **Microsoft Azure Storage Explorer** and click on the button that is highlighted in the following screenshot to connect to Azure Storage:

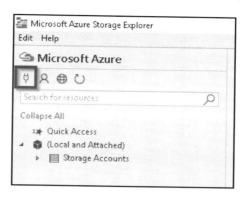

3. You will be prompted to enter a storage connection string, **shared access signature (SAS)**, or account key. For this recipe, let's use the storage connection string. Navigate to **Storage Account** and copy the connection string in the **Access Keys** blade and paste it in the **Connect to Azure Storage** popup, shown as follows:

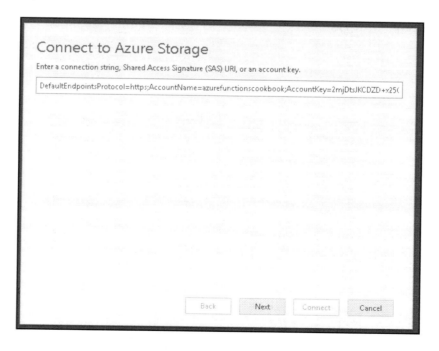

4. Clicking on the **Next** button in the preceding screenshot will take you to the **Connection Summary** window, which displays the account name and other related details for the confirmation. Click on the **Connect** button to get connected to the chosen Azure Storage account.

5. As shown in the following screenshot, you are now connected to the Azure Storage account, where you can manage all your Azure Storage services:

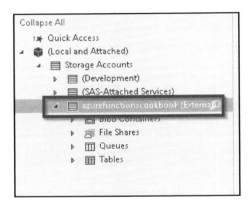

6. Now let's create a storage container named `samples-workitems`. Right-click on the `Blob Containers` folder and click on **Create Blob Container** to create a new Blob container named `samples-workitems`. Once the container is created, click on the **Upload files** button, as shown in the following screenshot:

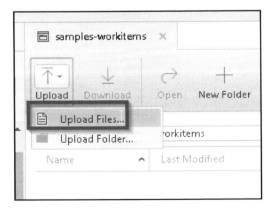

7. In the **Upload Files** window, choose a file that you would like to upload and click on the **Upload** window.

8. Immediately navigate to the Azure Function code editor and look at the **Logs** window, as shown in the following screenshot. The log shows the Azure Function getting triggered successfully:

```
Logs
2017-06-18T12:38:53  No new trace in the past 4 min(s).
2017-06-18T12:39:53  No new trace in the past 5 min(s).
2017-06-18T12:40:53  No new trace in the past 6 min(s).
2017-06-18T12:41:40.676 Function started (Id=1e0d5eaa-325c-465e-b8dd-20685f6b3734)
2017-06-18T12:41:40.676 C# Blob trigger function Processed blob
Name:EmployeeInfo.json
Size: 856 Bytes
2017-06-18T12:41:40.676 Function completed (Success, Id=1e0d5eaa-325c-465e-b8dd-20685f6b3734, Duration=2ms)
```

Testing Queue trigger using the Azure Management portal

1. Create a new Queue trigger named `QueueTriggerTestusingPortal`, as shown in the following screenshot. Note the Queue name `myqueue-items`. We need to create a Queue service with the same name later using the Azure Management portal:

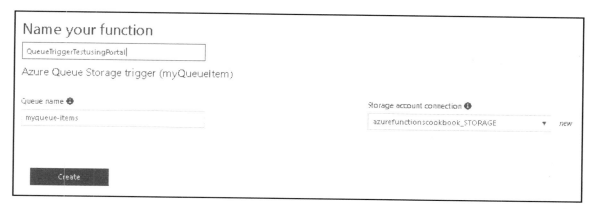

2. Navigate to the storage account's **Overview** blade and click on **Queues**, as shown in the following screenshot:

3. In the **Queue service** blade, click on **Queue** to add a new Queue:

4. Provide a Queue name as `myqueue-items` in the **Add queue** popup, as shown in the following screenshot, which we used while creating the Queue trigger. Click on **OK** to create the Queue service:

5. Once the Queue service is created, we need to create a Queue message. In the Azure Management portal, click on the Queue service **myqueue-items** to navigate to the **Messages** blade. Click on the **Add message** button, as shown in the following screenshot, provide a Queue message text, and click on **OK** to create the Queue message:

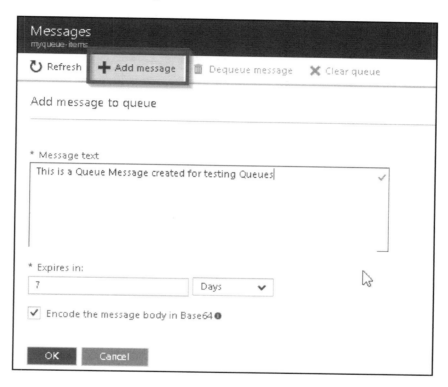

6. Immediately navigate to the Queue trigger **QueueTriggerTestusingPortal** and view the **Logs** blade to understand how the Queue function got triggered, as shown in the following screenshot:

```
Logs

2017-06-18T13:53:50  No new trace in the past 9 min(s).
2017-06-18T13:54:50  No new trace in the past 10 min(s).
2017-06-18T13:55:50  No new trace in the past 11 min(s).
2017-06-18T13:56:44.592 Function started (Id=dab4296e-ce42-4334-a779-5be81c1b02a2)
2017-06-18T13:56:44.592 C# Queue trigger function processed: This is a Queue Message created for testing Queues
2017-06-18T13:56:44.592 Function completed (Success, Id=dab4296e-ce42-4334-a779-5be81c1b02a2, Duration=0ms)
```

There's more...

For all your HTTP triggers, if you would like to allow your API consumers only the POST method, then you can restrict it by choosing **Selected methods** and choosing only **POST** in **Selected HTTP methods** , as shown in the following screenshot:

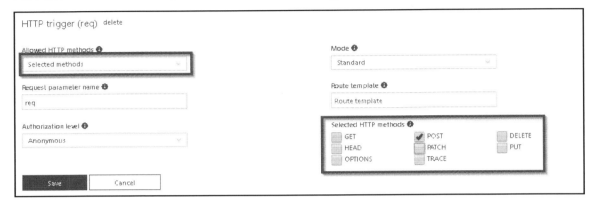

Testing an Azure Function on a staged environment using deployment slots

In general, every application would need preproduction environments such as staging, beta, and so on for reviewing the functionalities before publishing them for the end users.

Though the preproduction environments are great and help multiple stakeholders validate the application functionality against the business requirements, there are some pain points in managing and maintaining them. The following are a few of them:

- We would need to create a separate environment for setting them up
- Once everything is reviewed in preproduction and IT Ops team gets a go-ahead, there would be a bit of downtime in the production environment while deploying the code base of the new functionalities

All the preceding limitations can be covered in Azure Functions using a feature called **slots** (these are called **deployment slots** in App Service environments). Using slots, you can set up a preproduction environment where you can review all the new functionalities and promote them (by swapping, which we will discuss in a moment) to the production environment seamlessly whenever you need.

How to do it...

1. Create a new function app named MyProductionApp.

2. Create a new HTTP trigger and name it MyProd-HttpTrigger1. Please replace the last line with the following:

```
return name == null ?
 req.CreateResponse(HttpStatusCode.BadRequest, "Please pass a
 name on the query string or in the request body")
 : req.CreateResponse(HttpStatusCode.OK, "Welcome to MyProd-
 HttpTrigger1 of Production App " + name);
```

3. Create another new HTTP trigger and name it MyProd-HttpTrigger2. Use the same code that you used for MyProd-HttpTrigger1. Just replace the last line with the following.

```
return name == null ?
 req.CreateResponse(HttpStatusCode.BadRequest, "Please pass a
 name on the query string or in the request body")
 : req.CreateResponse(HttpStatusCode.OK, "Welcome to MyProd-
 HttpTrigger2 of Production App " + name);
```

4. Assume that both the functions of the function app are live on your production environment with the URL
   http://<<functionappname.azurewebsites.net>>.

5. Now, the customer has requested us to make some changes to both functions. Instead of directly making the changes to the functions of your production function app, you might need to create a slot.

6. Hold on! Before you can create a slot, you first need to enable the feature by navigating to the **Function app settings** under the **General Settings** of the **Platform features** tab of the function app, Once you click on the **Function app settings**, a new tab will be opened where you can enable the **Slots(preview)** as shown in the following screenshot:

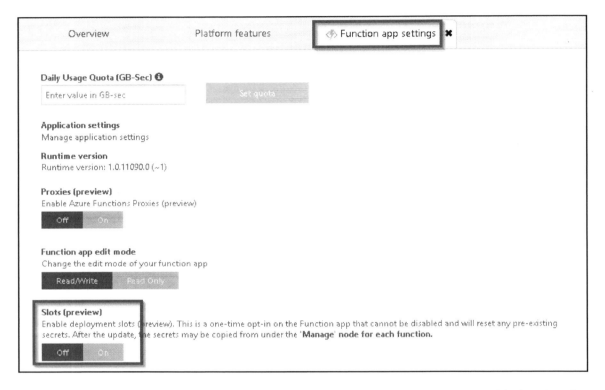

7. Click on the **ON** button available in the **Slots (preview)** section highlighted in the preceding screenshot. As soon as you turn it on, the slots section will be hidden as it is a one-time setting. Once it's enabled, you cannot disable it.

8. OK, let's create a new slot named `MyStagedApp` with all the functions that we have in our function app named `MyProductionApp`.

9. Click on the **+** icon available near the **Slots (preview)** section, as shown in the following screenshot:

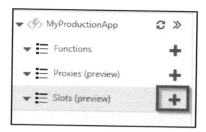

10. It prompts you to enter a name for the new slot. Provide a meaningful name something such as `Staging` , as shown in the following screenshot:

11. Once you click on **Create**, a new slot will be created, as shown in the following screenshot:

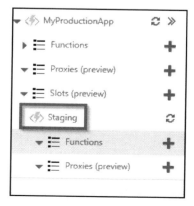

12. The URL for the slot will be
    `http://<<functionappname>>-<<Slotname>>.azurewebsites.net>>`.
    Each slot within a function app would have a different URL.

13. To make a staged environment complete, you need to copy all the Azure
    Functions from the production environment (in this case, the `MyProductionApp`
    app) to the new staged slot named `Staging`. Create two HTTP triggers and copy
    both the functions' code (`MyProd-HttpTrigger1` and `MyProd-HttpTrigger2`)
    from `MyProductionApp` to the new `Staging` slot. Basically, you need to copy all
    the functions to the new slot manually.

14. Replace the production app instances to staging app in the last line of both the
    functions in the **Staging** slot. This is useful for testing the output of the swap
    operation.

Note that in all the slots that you create as a preproduction app, you need to
make sure that you have the same Function names that you have in your
production environment.

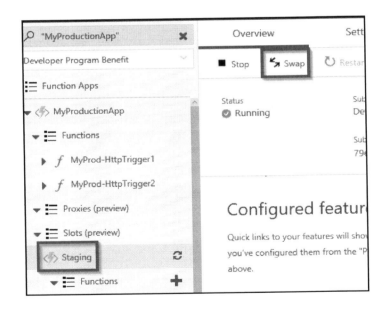

15. Click on the **Swap** button available in the **Deployment slots** blade, as shown in the following screenshot:

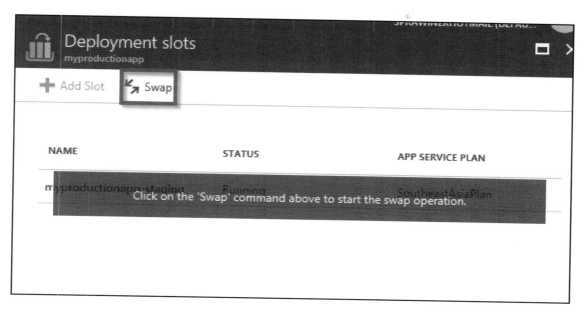

16. In the **Swap** blade, you need to choose the following:
    - **Swap Type**: Choose the **Swap** option.
    - **Source**: Choose the slot that you would like to move to production. In this case, **Staging** in general, you can even swap across non-production slots.

- **Destination**: Choose the **production** option, as shown in the following screenshot:

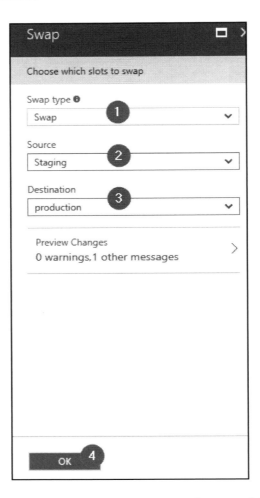

17. Once you review the settings, click on the **OK** button of the preceding step. It will take a few moments to swap the functions and a progress bar will appear, as shown in the following screenshot:

18. After a minute or two, the staging and production slots get swapped. Let's review the `run.csx` script files of the production:

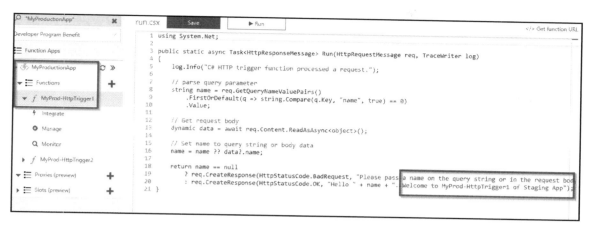

19. If you don't see any changes, click on the refresh button of the function app, as shown in the following screenshot:

20. Be cautious that the **Application settings** and **Database Connection Strings** are marked as **Slot Setting** (slot-specific). Otherwise, **Application settings** and **Database Connection Strings** will also get swapped, which could cause unexpected behavior. You can mark any of these settings from **Platform features**, as shown in the following figure:

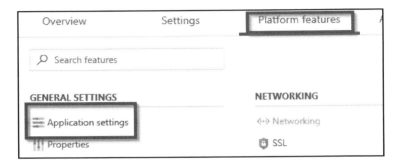

21. Clicking on the **Application settings** will take you to the following blade, where you can mark any setting as a Slot setting:

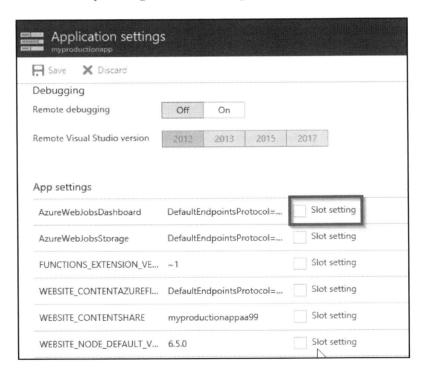

All the functions taken in the recipe are HTTP triggers; note that you can have any kind of triggers in the function app. The deployment slots are not limited to HTTP triggers.

You can have multiple slots for each of your function apps. The following are few of the examples:

- Alpha
- Beta
- Staging

You need to have all the Azure Functions in each of the slots that you would like to swap with your production function app:

- Slots are specific to the function app but not to the individual function.
- Once you enable the slots features, all the keys will be regenerated, including the master. Be cautious if you have already shared the keys of the functions with third parties. If you have already shared them and enabled the slots, all the existing integrations with the old keys wouldn't work.

In general, if you are using App Services and would like to create deployment slots, you need to have your App Service plan in either one of the Standard or Premium tiers. However, you can create slots for the function app even if it is in Consumption (or dynamic) plans.

There's more

If you try to create a slot without enabling the feature, you will see something similar to what is shown in the following screenshot:

Load testing Azure Functions using VSTS

Every application needs to perform well in terms of performance. It's everyone's responsibility within the team that the application is performing well. In this recipe, you will learn how to create a load on the Azure Functions using the load test tool provided by VSTS. This recipe will also help you understand how the auto-scaling of instances works in the serverless environment without the developers or architect worrying about the instances that are responsible for serving the requests.

Getting ready

Create a VSTS account at `https://www.visualstudio.com/`. We will be using the load test tool of VSTS to create URL-based load testing.

How to do it...

1. Create a new HTTP trigger named `LoadTestHttpTrigger` with **Authorization Level** set to **Anonymous**.

2. Replace the default code with the following in `run.csx`:

```
using System.Net;
public static async Task<HttpResponseMessage>
Run(HttpRequestMessage req, TraceWriter log)
{
    System.Threading.Thread.Sleep(2000);
    return req.CreateResponse(HttpStatusCode.OK, "Hello ");
}
```

3. The preceding code is self-explainable. In order to make the load test interesting, let's simulate some processing load by adding a wait time of two seconds using `System.Threading.Thread.Sleep(2000);`.

4. Copy the function URL by clicking on the **</> Get function URL** link available on the right-hand side of the `run.csx` code editor, as shown in the following screenshot:

5. Navigate to **Load test** tab of the VSTS account.

6. Click on **New** link and select **URL based test**, as shown in the following screenshot:

7. In the **Web Scenarios** tab, provide a meaningful name for the load test, as shown in the following screenshot:

8. Paste the HTTP trigger URL that you have copied in *step 4* into the **URL** input field, as shown in the following screenshot:

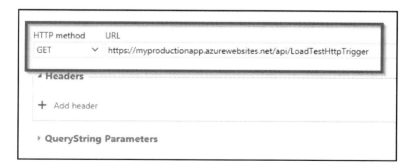

9. Now, click on the **Save** button to save the load test:

10. The next step is to provide details about the load that we would like to create on the Azure Function. As shown in the following screenshot, click on **Settings** and provide the details about the load test that you would like depending on your requirements:

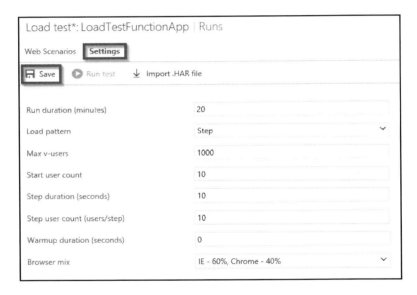

11. Click on **Save** once you provide all your details for the load test. Once you save the test, the **Run test** button will be enabled, as shown in the following screenshot:

12. Click on **Run test** to start the load test. As the run duration of our load test is 20 minutes, it would take 20 minutes to complete the load test. Once the load is complete, VSTS provides us with the performance reports, shown as follows:
    - **Summary Report**: This provides us the average response time of the HTTP trigger for the load of **1K users**.

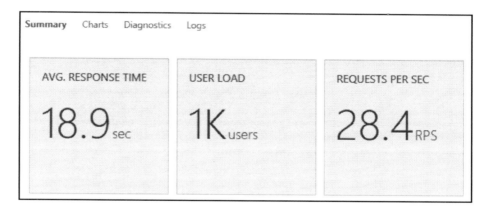

- **Performance reports**: The following performance report provides us with insights of how the application is behaving as we keep the load growing:

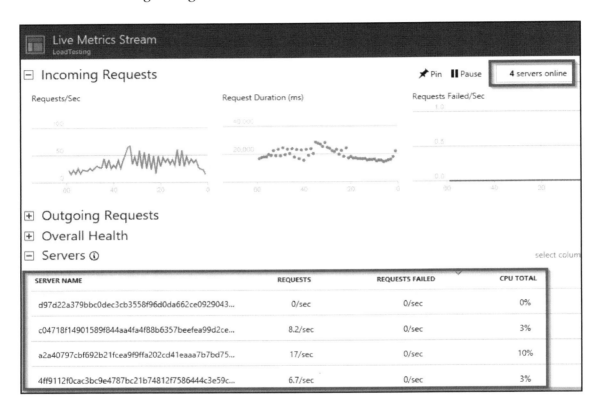

There's more...

We can also look at how Azure scales out the instances automatically behind the scenes in the **Live Metrics Stream** tab of **Application Insights**. The following screenshot shows the instance IDs and the health of the virtual machines that are allocated automatically based on the load on the Azure serverless architecture. You will learn how to integrate Application Insights with Azure Functions in Chapter 6, *Monitoring and Troubleshooting Azure Serverless Services*:

See also

- The *Monitoring Azure Functions using Application Insights* recipe in Chapter 6, *Monitoring and Troubleshooting Azure Serverless Services*

Creating and testing Azure Function locally using Azure CLI tools

Most of the recipes that you have learned so far have been created either using the browser or using Visual Studio **Integrated Development Environment (IDE)**.

Azure also provides us with tools that help developers who love working with the command line. These tools allow us to create Azure resources right from the command line with simple commands. In this recipe, you will learn how to create a new function app and also understand how to create a function and deploy it to the Azure Cloud right from the command line.

Getting ready

1. Install Node.js from `https://nodejs.org/en/download/`.
2. Once you install Node.js, you need to install the Azure Function Core Tools npm package. Navigate to your Command Prompt and run the following command:

   ```
   npm i -g azure-functions-core-tools
   ```

3. As shown in the following screenshot, the tools related to Azure Functions will get installed:

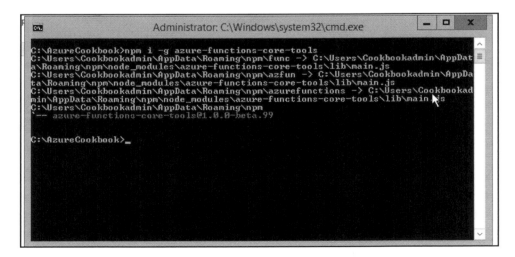

How to do it...

1. Once the Azure Functions Core Tools are ready, run the following command to create a new function app:

```
func init
```

   You will get the following output after executing the preceding command:

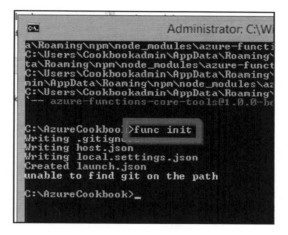

Just ignore the `unable to find the git in the path` error, as we are not going to use Git in the recipe.

2. Run the following command to create a new HTTP trigger function within the new function app that we have created:

```
func new
```

You will get the following output after executing the preceding command:

3. You will be prompted to choose the language in which you would like to code. As shown in the preceding screenshot, I have chosen C#. Once you are ready, press *Enter* to go to the next step.

4. You will now be prompted to select the function template. For this recipe, I have chosen HttpTrigger, as shown in the following screenshot. Choose HttpTrigger by using the down arrow. You can choose the Azure Function type based on your requirement. You can navigate between the options using the up/down arrows available on your keyboard:

5. The next step is to provide a name to the Azure Function that you are creating. Provide a meaningful name and press Enter, as shown in the following screenshot:

```
C:\AzureCookbook>func new
Select a language: C#

Function name: [HttpTriggerCSharp] HttpTrigger-CoreTools
Writing C:\AzureCookbook\HttpTrigger-CoreTools\run.csx
Writing C:\AzureCookbook\HttpTrigger-CoreTools\sample.dat
Writing C:\AzureCookbook\HttpTrigger-CoreTools\function.json

C:\AzureCookbook>_
```

6. You can use your favorite IDE to edit the Azure Function code. In this recipe, I am using Visual Studio Code to open the HttpTrigger function, as shown in the following screenshot:

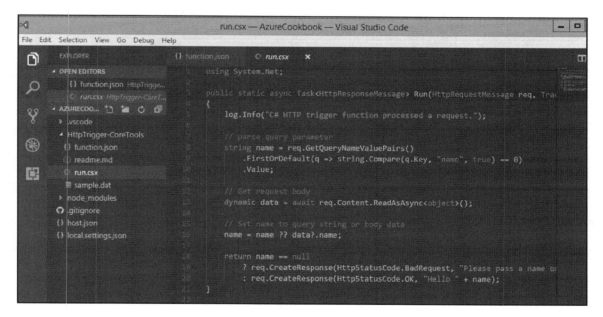

7. Let's test the Azure Function right from your local machine. For this, we need to start the Azure Function host by running the following command:

```
func host start
```

8. Once the host is started, you can copy the URL (which is highlighted in the preceding screenshot) and test it in your browser along with a query string parameter name, as shown in the following screenshot:

Testing and validating Azure Function responsiveness using Application Insights

Any application is useful for any business only if it up and running. Applications might go down for multiple reasons, and the following are a few of them:

- Any hardware failures such as server crash, bad hard disk, or any other hardware, or even an entire data center might go down, which might be very rare
- There might be any software errors because of bad code or a deployment error
- The site might receive unexpected traffic and the servers may not be capable of handling the traffic
- There might be cases where your application is accessible from one country but not the others

It would be really helpful if we can get any notification if our site is not available or not responding to the user requests. Azure provides a few tools for us to help in alerting if the website is not responding or is down. One of them is Application Insights. You will learn how to configure Application Insights that ping our Azure Function app for every minute and alert us if the Function is not responding.

Getting ready

1. Navigate to Azure Management portal, click on **New** , and then select **Monitoring + Management**. Choose **Application Insights** and provide all the required details, as shown in the following screenshot:

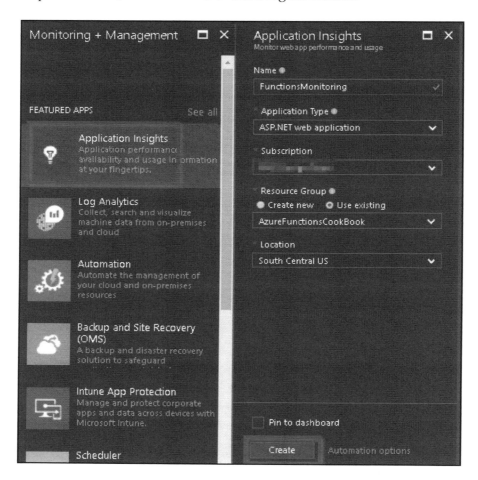

2. Once you review, click on the **Create** button to create the Application Insights.

3. Navigate to your function app's **Overview** blade and grab the function app **URL**, as shown in the following screenshot:

How to do it...

1. Navigate to the **Availability** blade and click on **Add test** button, as shown in the following screenshot:

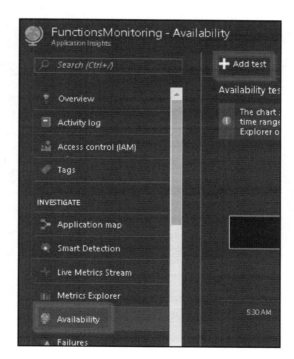

2. In the **Create test** blade, enter a meaningful name for your requirement and paste the function app URL that you have noted down in the **URL** field of the **Create test** blade. In the **Alerts** blade, provide a valid email address in the **Send alert emails to these email addresses:** field to which an alert should be sent if the function is not available or not responding:

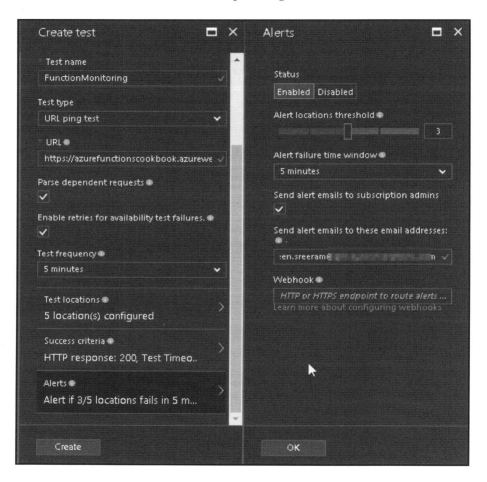

3. Click on **OK** in the **Alerts** blade and then click on the **Create** button of the **Create test** blade to create the test, as shown in the following screenshot in the **All availability tests** section:

4. In order to test the functionality of this alert, let's stop the function app by clicking on the **Stop** button available in the **Overview** tab of the function app, as shown in the following screenshot:

5. When the function app was stopped, Application Insights will try to access the function URL using the ping test and the response code will not be 200 as the app was stopped, which means the test failed and a notification was sent to the configured email, as shown in the following screenshot:

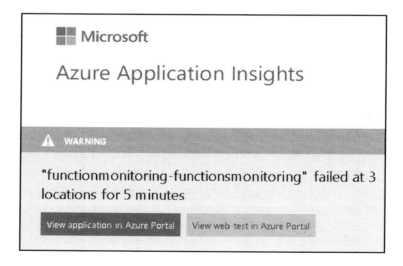

How it works...

We have created an `Availability` test where our function app will be pinged once every five minutes from a maximum of five different locations across the world. You can configure them in the **Test Location** tab of the **Create test** blade while creating the test. The default criterion of the ping is to check whether the response code of the URL is `200`. If the response code is not `200`, then the test has failed, and an alert is sent to the configurable email address.

There's more...

You can use multi-step web test (using the **Test Type** option in the **Create test** blade) if you would like to test a page or functionality that requires navigating to multiple pages.

6

Monitoring and Troubleshooting Azure Serverless Services

In this chapter, you will learn the following:

- Monitoring your Azure Functions
- Monitoring Azure Functions using Application Insights
- Pushing custom telemetry details to analytics of Application Insights
- Sending application telemetry details via email
- Integrating real-time Application Insights monitoring data with Power BI using Azure Functions

Introduction

Completing the development of the project and making the application live is not the end of the story. We need to continuously monitor the application, analyze the performance, and review the logs to understand whether there are any issues that end users are facing. Azure provides us with multiple tools to achieve all the monitoring requirements right from the development stage and the maintenance stage of the application.

In this chapter, you will learn how to utilize this information and take necessary actions based on the information available.

Monitoring your Azure Functions

In this recipe, you will learn the following:

- Individual function logs:
    - Reviewing the logs in the **Logs** section located below the code editor of the Azure Functions in the Azure Management portal
    - Reviewing the execution log in the **Monitor** tab of the Azure Function
- All functions of a given function app:
    - Log streaming

Getting ready

1. Navigate to the **Platform features** of the function app and click on **Diagnostic Logs** blade, as shown in the following screenshot:

2. In the **Logs** blade, enable **Application Logging (Filesystem)** by clicking on the **On** button, as shown in the following screenshot if it is **Off**. And then, click on **Save** to save the changes:

How to do it...

1. Navigate to the code editor in the Azure Management portal of any Azure Function. You will notice a bar at the bottom with the title **Logs**. Click on the bar to expand it. After expanding, it should look like what is shown in the following screenshot, where you can view all the logs that show the events that happen after you open it:

```
Logs

2017-06-19T15:53:27  Welcome, you are now connected to log-streaming service.
2017-06-19T15:54:27  No new trace in the past 1 min(s).
2017-06-19T15:55:27  No new trace in the past 2 min(s).
```

2. Let's navigate to **Monitor** tab to view all the past events that happened with the Azure Function. The following is the list of events that happened in the `RegisterUser` function that we created in our previous chapters:

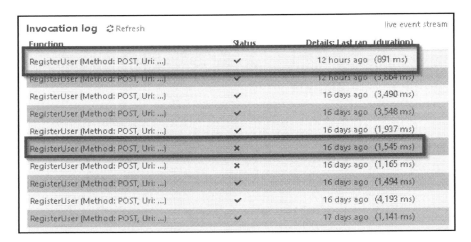

3. Click on any of the log items for which the **Status** is a success. As shown in the following screenshot, you will see all the request and binding details of the particular event that happened with this function:

4. Let's now click on any of the log item for which the status column indicates failure. You will see the request and binding details along with a special field named **Failure** that provides details about the reason for the failure. Detailed error details are available in the **Logs** section of the following screenshot:

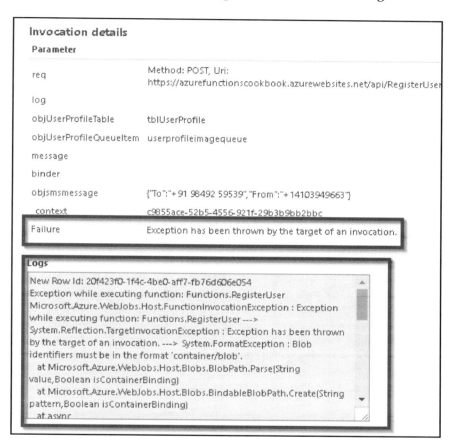

5. In order to view live data of the events, navigate to the **Platform features** tab of the function app and click on **Log streaming** , shown as follows:

6. Clicking on the **Log streaming** link in the preceding screenshot will take you to the **Streaming logs** window, where you can view all the events happening in all the functions of the selected function app:

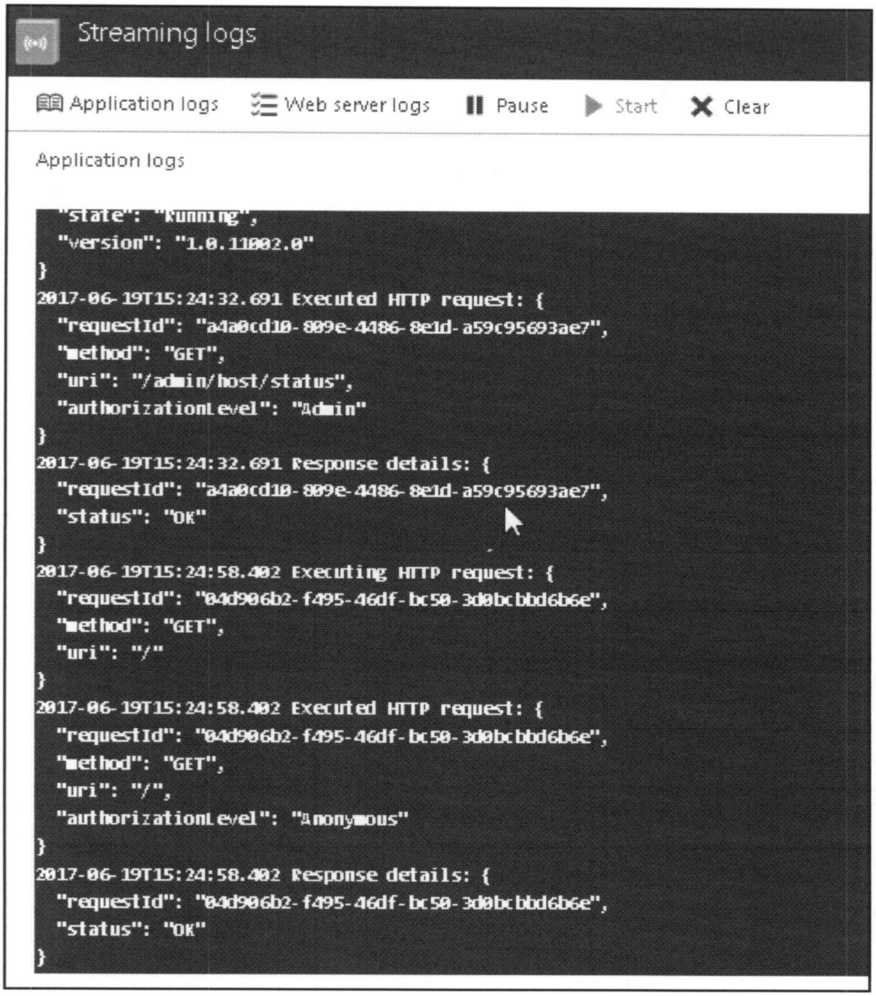
Streaming logs
Application logs
Web server logs
Pause
Start
Clear
Application logs
"version": "1.0.11002.0"
}
2017-06-19T15:24:32.691 Executed HTTP request: {
"requestId": "a4a0cd10-809e-4486-8e1d-a59c95693ae7",
"method": "GET",
"uri": "/admin/host/status",
"authorizationLevel": "Admin"
}
2017-06-19T15:24:32.691 Response details: {
"requestId": "a4a0cd10-809e-4486-8e1d-a59c95693ae7",
"status": "OK"
}
2017-06-19T15:24:58.402 Executing HTTP request: {
"requestId": "04d906b2-f495-46df-bc50-3d0bcbbd6b6e",
"method": "GET",
"uri": "/"
}
2017-06-19T15:24:58.402 Executed HTTP request: {
"requestId": "04d906b2-f495-46df-bc50-3d0bcbbd6b6e",
"method": "GET",
"uri": "/",
"authorizationLevel": "Anonymous"
}
2017-06-19T15:24:58.402 Response details: {
"requestId": "04d906b2-f495-46df-bc50-3d0bcbbd6b6e",
"status": "OK"
}

There's more...

Each function event is logged in an Azure Storage Table service. Every month, a table is created with the name `AzureWebJobsHostLogs<Year><Month>`.

As part of troubleshooting any error, if you would like to get more details of any error, you first get the **_context** field available in the **Invocation details** section and look up that data in **RowKey** of the **AzureWebJobsHostLogs** table.

Monitoring Azure Functions using Application Insights

Application Insights (AI) is an application performance management service that helps us in monitoring the performance of an application hosted anywhere. Once you integrate AI into your application, it will start sending telemetry data to your AI account hosted on the cloud. In this recipe, you will learn how simple is it to integrate Azure Functions with AI

Getting ready

We created an AI account in the *Testing and validating Azure Function responsiveness using Application Insights* recipe of `Chapter 5`, *Exploring Testing Tools for the Validation of Azure Functions*. Create one, if not created already, using the following steps:

1. Navigate to Azure Management portal, click on **New** , and then select **Monitoring + Management**,. Choose **Application Insights** and provide all the required details, as shown in the following screenshot:

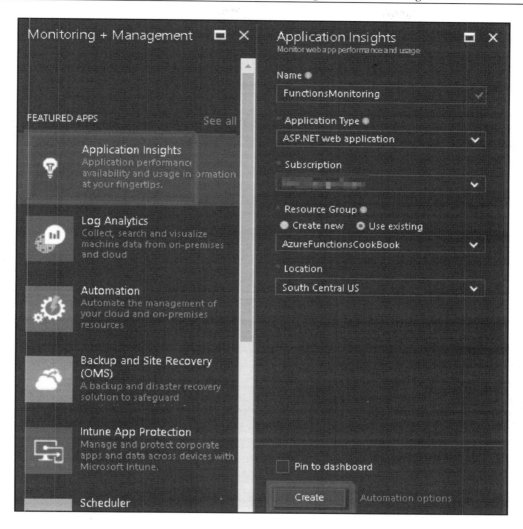

2. Once you review, click on the **Create** button to create the AI.

How to do it...

1. Once the AI account is created, navigate to the Overview tab and grab **Instrumentation Key** , as shown in the following screenshot:

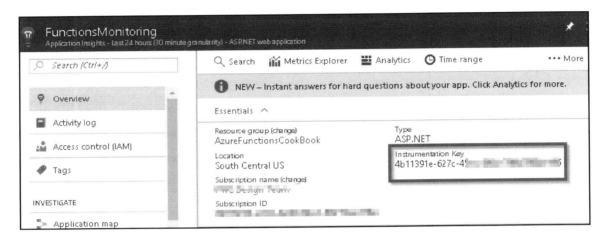

2. Navigate to **Function Apps** for which you would like to enable monitoring and go to **Application settings** , as shown in the following screenshot:

3. Add a new key with the name `APPINSIGHTS_INSTRUMENTATIONKEY` and provide the instrumentation key that you have copied from the AI account, shown as follows, and click on **Save** to save the changes:

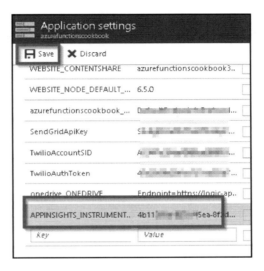

4. If everything goes fine, you will see the **Application Insights** link in the **Configured features** section, as shown in the following screenshot:

5. That's it; you can start utilizing all the features of AI to monitor the performance of your Azure Functions. Open **Application Insights** and the `RegisterUser` function in two different tabs to test how **Live Metrics Stream** works:

   1. Open **Application Insights** and click on **Live Metrics Stream** in the first tab of your browser, as shown in the following screenshot:

   2. Open the `RegisterUser` function in another tab and run a few tests.

6. After you have completed the tests, go to the tab that has AI. You should see the live traffic coming to your function app, as shown in the following screenshot:

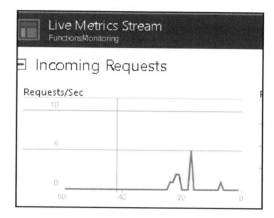

How it works...

We have created an AI account. Once you integrate AI's **Instrumentation Key** with the Azure Function, the runtime will take care of sending the telemetry data asynchronously to your AI account hosted on Azure.

There's more ...

In **Live Metrics Stream**, you can also view all the instances along with some other data, such as the number of requests per second handled by your instances.

Pushing custom telemetry details to analytics of Application Insights

We have been asked by our customers to provide analytic reports of a derived metric with in AI. So, what is a derived metric? Well, by default, AI provides you with many insights about the metrics like requests, errors, exceptions, and so on. You can run queries on the information that AI provide using AI - Analytics query language, say, if you would like to understand the number of requests that are coming to a website for every hour a new metric derived from the out of the box metric.

In this context, `requests per hour` is a derived metric) and if you would like to build a new report within AI then you need to feed AI about the new derived metric on a regular basis. Once you feed the required data regularly, AI will take care of providing the reports for our analysis.

We will be using Azure Functions that feed the AI with a derived metric named `requests per hour`:

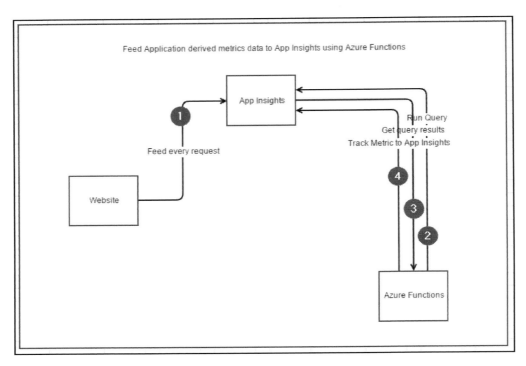

For this example, we will develop a query using Analytics query language for the `request per hour` derived metric. You can make changes to the query to generate other derived metrics for your requirement, say, *requests per hour for my campaign* or something similar to that.

You can learn more about Analytics query language at `https://docs.microsoft.com/en-us/azure/application-insights/app-insights-analytics-reference`.

Getting ready

- Create a new AI account if you don't have one already.
- Make sure you have a running application that integrates with the AI. You can learn how to integrate your application with AI at `https://docs.microsoft.com/en-us/azure/application-insights/app-insights-asp-net`.

How to do it...

We will perform the following steps to pushing custom telemetry details to analytics of Application Insights.

Creating AI function

Create a new function template by choosing **Monitoring** in the **Scenario** drop-down, as shown in the following screenshot:

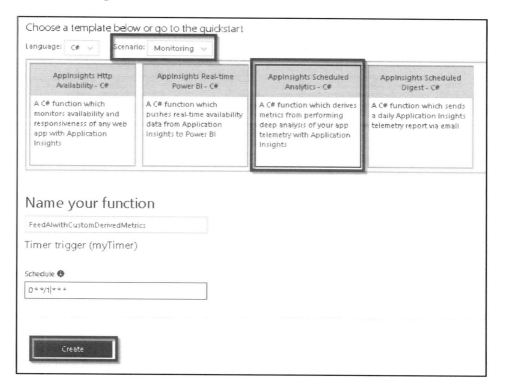

Configuring access keys

1. Click on **Create** to create the function and navigate to AI's **Overview** blade, as shown, and copy the **Instrumentation Key.** Now, in the Azure Function App, create new app setting with the name AI_IKEY and use the Instrumentation Key as the value for the AI_IKEY setting:

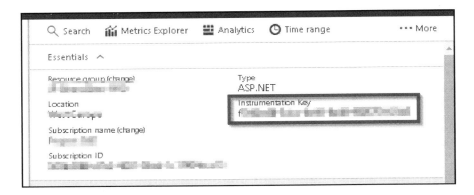

2. Navigate to **API Access** blade, copy the **Application ID**, and create new app setting with the name AI_APP_ID:

3. We also need to create a new API key. As shown in the preceding step, click on the **Create API key** button to generate the new API key, as shown in the following screenshot. Provide a meaningful name, check the **Read telemetry** data, and click on **Generate key**:

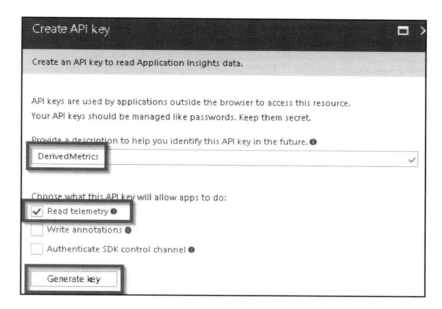

4. Once the **Generate key** is clicked on, you can view and copy the key, as shown in the following screenshot. And then, create new app setting with the name `AI_APP_KEY`:

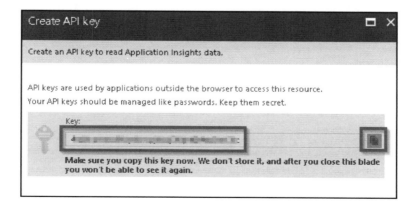

5. You might have already created the following **Application settings** in the Azure Function app. If not, create three **App setting** keys, as shown in the following screenshot. All these three keys will be used in our Azure Function named as FeedAIwithCustomDerivedMetrics:

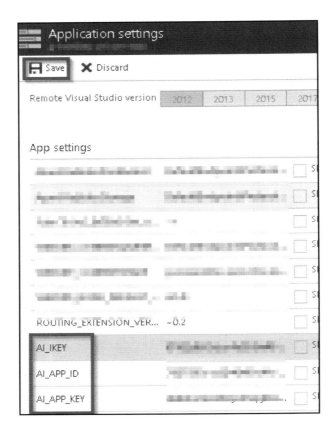

Integrating and testing AI query

1. Now, it's time to develop the query that provides us with the derived metric value `requests per hour`. Navigate to the AI **Overview** blade and click on the **Analytics** button, as shown in the following screenshot:

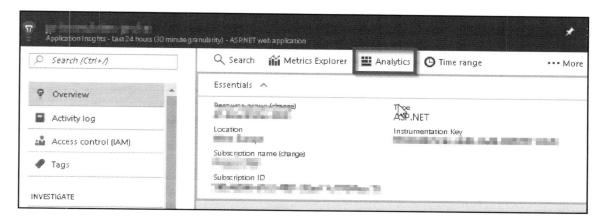

2. You will be taken to the analytics website, as shown in the following screenshot. Click on the new tab icon where we write the query to pull the required data to derive our custom metric:

3. Write the following query in the new query tab. You can write your own query as per your requirements. Make sure that the query returns a scalar value:

```
requests
| where timestamp > now(-1h)
| summarize count()
```

4. Once you are done with your query, run it by clicking on the **Go** button to see the count of records, as shown in the following screenshot:

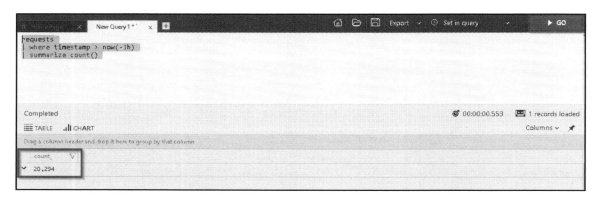

5. We are now ready with the required AI query. Let's integrate the query with our `FeedAIwithCustomDerivedMetrics` function. Navigate to the Azure Function code editor and make the following changes:

   1. Provide a meaningful name for our derived metric, in this case, `Requests per hour`.
   2. Replace the default query with the one that we have developed.
   3. Save the changes by clicking on the **Save** button:

```
29  public static async Task Run(TimerInfo myTimer, TraceWriter log)
30  {
31      if (myTimer.IsPastDue)
32      {
33          log.Warning($"[Warning]: Timer is running late! Last ran
34      }
35
36      // [CONFIGURATION_REQUIRED] update the query accordingly for
37      // be sure to run it against Application Insights Analytics p
38      // output should be a number if sending derived metrics
39      // [Application Insights Analytics] https://docs.microsoft.co
40      aw
41          name: "Requests per hour",
42          query: "
43  requests
44      | where timestamp > now(-1h)
45      | summarize count()
46      ",
47          log: log
48      );
49  }
```

6. Let's do a quick test to see whether you have configured all three app settings and the query correctly. Navigate to the **Integrate** tab and change the run frequency to one minute, as shown in the following screenshot:

7. Now, let's navigate to the **Monitor** tab and see whether everything is working fine. If there are any problem, you will see a **X** mark in the **Status** column. View the error in the **Logs** section in the **Monitor** tab by clicking on the **Invocation log** entry:

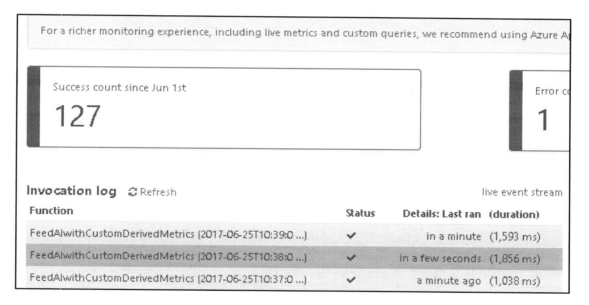

8. Once you make sure that the function is running smoothly, revert the **Schedule** frequency to one hour.

Configuring the custom derived metric report

1. Navigate to the AI's **Overview** tab and click on **Metrics Explorer**, as shown in the following screenshot:

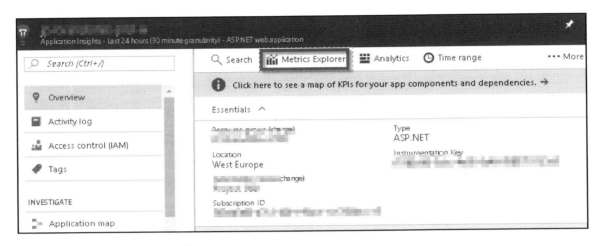

2. **Metrics Explorer** is where you will find all your analytics related to different metrics. In **Metrics Explorer**, click on the **Edit** button located in any report to configure our custom metric, as shown in the following screenshot:

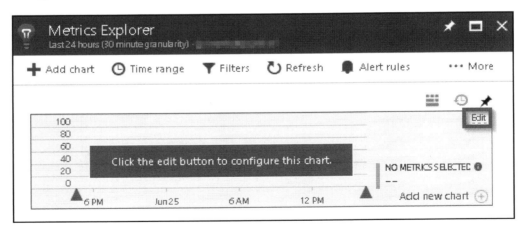

3. After clicking on the **Edit** button, you will be taken to the **Chart details** blade, where you can configure your custom metric and all other details related to the chart. In the **Metrics** section, search for your custom metric name like I did, as shown in the following screenshot, and click on it:

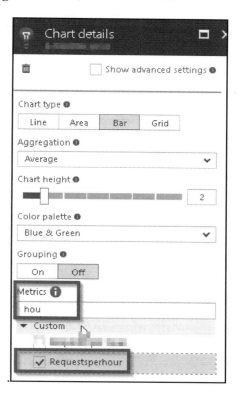

 If you don't see your custom metric under **Custom** section, as shown in the preceding screenshot, change the time range values as per the time you ran your Azure Function.

4. That's it; the report will start showing the data as per your configuration. This is what it looks like as soon as you check your Metric:

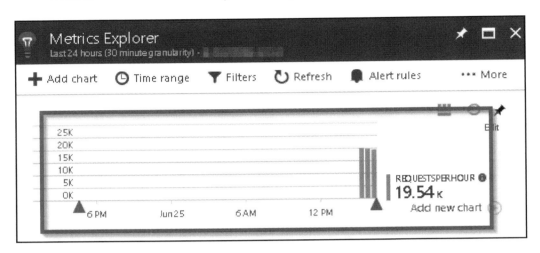

How it works...

This is how the entire process works:

- We have created the Azure Function using the default Delete repeated word
- We have configured the following keys in the **Application Settings** of the Azure Function app:
    - AI's **Instrumentation Key**
    - The application ID
    - The API access key
- The Azure Function runtime will automatically consume the AI API, run the custom query to retrieve the required metrics, and perform the required operations of feeding the derived telemetry data to AI.
- Once everything in the Azure Function is configured, we develop a simple query that pulls the request count of the last 1 hour and feed ir to the AI as a custom derived metric. This process repeats every 1 hour.
- Later, we configure a new report using **Metrics Explorer** of AI with our custom derived metric.

See also

- The *Integrating Azure Functions using Application Insights* recipe
- The *Sending application telemetry details via email* recipe

Sending application telemetry details via email

One of the post-live activities of your application would be to receive a notification email about the details of the health, errors, response time, and so on at least once a day.

Azure Function provide us with the ability to get all the basic details using a function template with the code that's is responsible for retrieving all the required values from the AI and the plumbing code of framing the email body and sending the email using SendGrid. We will look at how to do that in this recipe.

Getting ready

1. Create a new SendGrid account if you have not yet created one and get the SendGrid API key.
2. Create a new AI account if you don't have one already.
3. Make sure you have a running application that integrates with the AI.

 You can learn how to integrate your application with AI at `https://docs.microsoft.com/en-us/azure/application-insights/app-insights-asp-net`.

How to do it...

1. Create a new function by choosing **Monitoring** in the **Scenario** dropdown and select the **AppInsights Scheduled Digest - C#** template, as shown in the following screenshot:

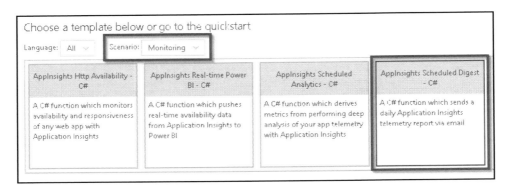

2. Once you select the template, you will be prompted to provide the name of the function, scheduled frequency, and **SendGrid API Key** for the SendGrid output binding, as shown in the following screenshot:

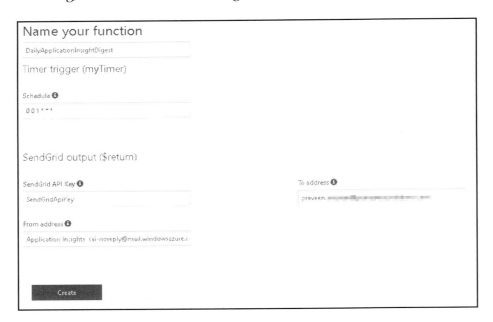

3. Once you review all the details, click on the **Create** button of the previous step to create the new Azure Function. The template creates all the code that is required to query the data from AI and send an email to the person mentioned in the **To address** of the preceding screenshot.

 Make sure that you follow the steps mentioned in *Configuring access keys* section of the *Pushing custom telemetry details to analytics of Application Insights* recipe to configure these access keys: AI **Instrumentation Key**, the application ID, and the API access key.

4. Navigate to the `run.csx` function and change the app name to your application name, as shown in the following screenshot:

```
// [CONFIGURATION_REQUIRED] configure {appName} accordingly for your app/email
string appName = "Azure Function Serverless Cookbook";
```

5. If you have configured all the setting properly, you will start receiving an email based on the timer settings.

6. Let's do a quick test run by clicking on the **Run** button available above the code editor, as shown in the following screenshot:

7. This is the screenshot of the email that I received after clicking on the **Run** button of the preceding screenshot:

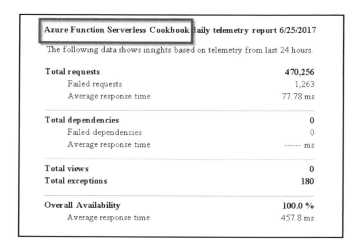

How it works...

The Azure Function uses the AI API to run all the AI analytics queries, retrieves all the results, frames the email body with all the details, and invokes the SendGrid API to send an email to the configured email account.

There's more...

Azure templates provide the default code that has a few queries that are in general useful in monitoring the application health. If you have any specific requirement of getting notification alerts, go ahead and add new queries to the GetQueryString method. In order to incorporate the new values, you would also need to change the DigestResult class and the GetHtmlContentValue function.

See also

- The *Sending an email notification to the administrator of the website using the SendGrid service* recipe of Chapter 2, *Working with Notifications Using SendGrid and Twilio Services*

Integrating real-time AI monitoring data with Power BI using Azure Functions

Sometimes, you would need to view some real-time data of your application availability or any information related to your application health on a custom website. Retrieving the information for the AI and displaying it in a custom report would be a tedious job as you need to develop a separate website and build, test, and host it somewhere.

In this recipe, you will learn how easy is to view real-time health information of the application by integrating AI and Power BI. We will be leveraging Power BI capabilities for live streaming of the data and Azure timer functions to continuous feed health information to Power BI. This is a high-level diagram of what we will be doing in the rest of the recipe:

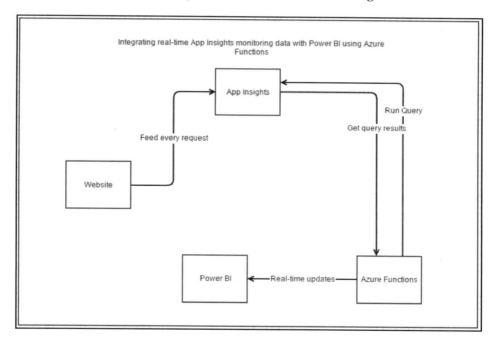

 Please make sure that you follow the steps mentioned in *Configuring access keys* section of the *Pushing custom telemetry details to analytics of Application Insights* recipe to configure these access keys: AI **Instrumentation Key**, the application ID, and the API access key.

Getting ready

1. Create a Power BI account at `https://powerbi.microsoft.com/en-us/`.
2. Create a new AI account if you don't have one already.
3. Make sure that you have a running application that integrates with the AI. You can learn how to integrate your application with AI at `https://docs.microsoft.com/en-us/azure/application-insights/app-insights-asp-net`.

How to do it...

We will perform the following steps to integrate AI and Power BI.

Configuring Power BI with dashboard, dataset, and push URI

1. If you are using the Power BI portal for the first time, you might have to click on **Skip for now** on the welcome page, as shown in the following screenshot:

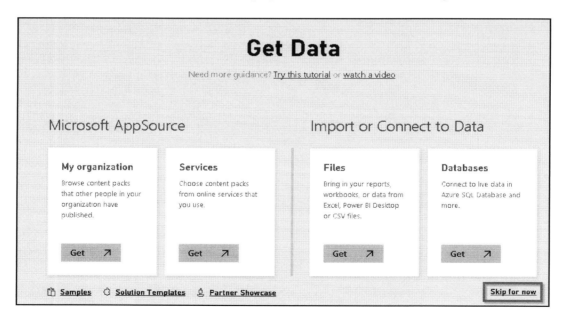

2. The next step is to create a streaming dataset by clicking on **Create** and then choosing **Streaming dataset**, as shown in the following screenshot:

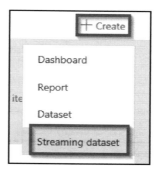

3. In the **New streaming dataset** step, select **API** and click on the **Next** button, as shown in the following screenshot:

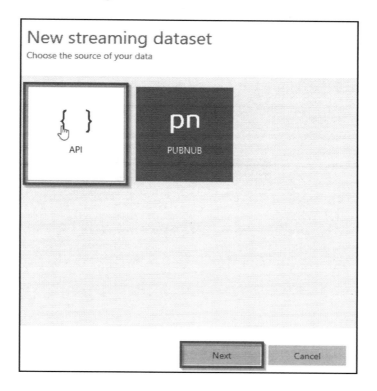

4. In the next step, you need to create the fields of the streaming dataset. Provide a meaningful name to the dataset and provide the values that you would like to push to Power BI. For this recipe, I have created a dataset with just one field named `RequestsPerSecond` of type **Number** and clicked on **Create** , as shown in the following screenshot:

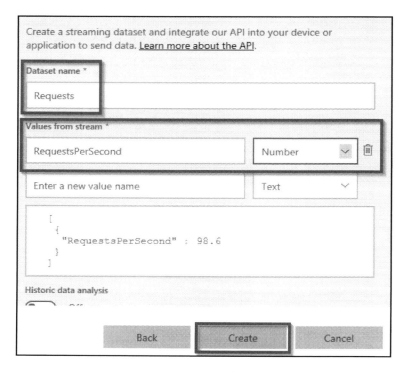

5. Once you create the dataset, you will be prompted with a **Push URL** as shown in the following screenshot. You will be using this **Push URL** in the Azure Functions to push the `RequestsPerSecond` data every 1 second (or depending on your requirements) with the actual value of request per second. Click on **Done**.

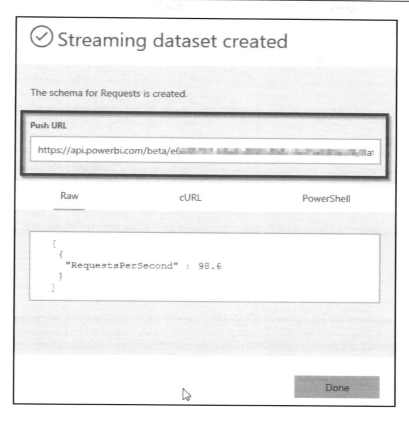

6. The next step is to create a dashboard along with a tile in it. Let's create a new dashboard by clicking on **Create** and choosing **Dashboard** , as shown in the following screenshot:

7. In the **Create dashboard** popup, provide a meaningful name and click on **Create**, as shown in the following screenshot, to create an empty dashboard:

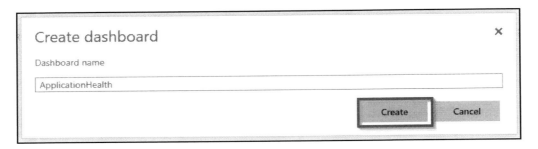

8. In the empty dashboard, click on the **Add tile** button to create a new tile. Clicking on **Add tile** will open a new popup, where you can select the data source from which the tile should be populated:

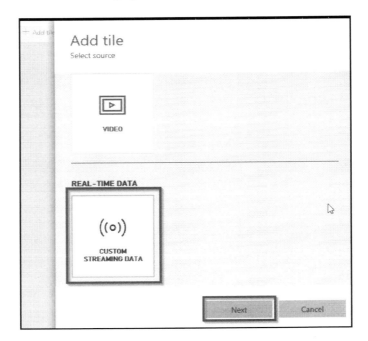

9. Select **CUSTOM STREAMING DATA** and click on **Next**, as shown in the preceding screenshot. In the following step, select the **Requests** dataset and click on the **Next** button:

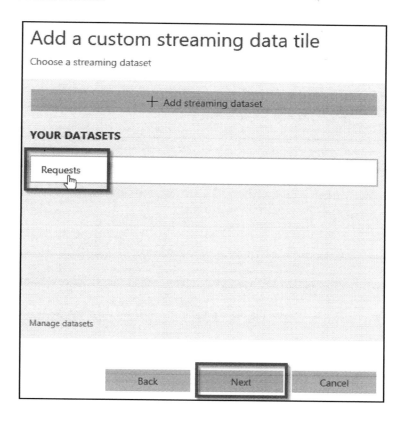

10. The next step is to choose **Visualization type** (it is `Card` in this case) and select the fields from the data source, as shown in the following screenshot:

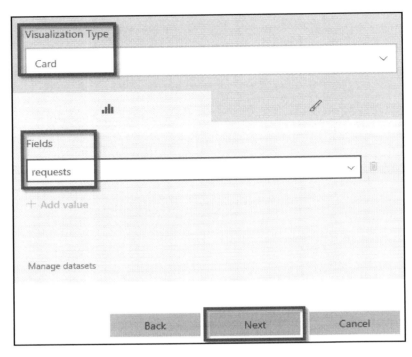

11. The final step is to provide a name to your tile. I have provided requests per second. The name might not make sense in this case. But you are free to provide any name as per your requirements.

Creating Azure AI real-time Power BI - C# function

To create Azure AI real-time Power BI using the C# function, complete the following steps:

1. Navigate to Azure Functions and create a new function using the following template:

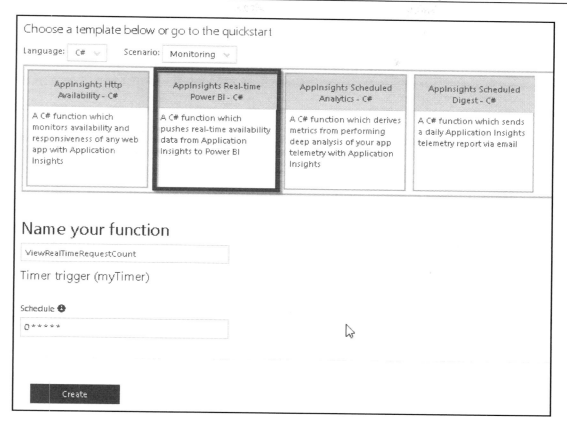

2. Replace the default code with the following code. Make sure that you configure the right value for which the analytics query should pull the data. In my case, I have provided five minutes (5m) in the following code:

```
#r "Newtonsoft.Json"
using System.Configuration;
using System.Text;
using Newtonsoft.Json.Linq;
private const string AppInsightsApi =
  "https://api.applicationinsights.io/beta/apps";
private const string RealTimePushURL = "PastethePushURLhere";
private static readonly string AiAppId =
  ConfigurationManager.AppSettings["AI_APP_ID"];
private static readonly string AiAppKey =
  ConfigurationManager.AppSettings["AI_APP_KEY"];

public static async Task Run(TimerInfo myTimer, TraceWriter
  log)
```

```
{
   if (myTimer.IsPastDue)
   {
      log.Warning($"[Warning]: Timer is running late! Last ran
       at: {myTimer.ScheduleStatus.Last}");
   }
   await RealTimeFeedRun(
   query: @"
   requests
   | where timestamp > ago(5m)
   | summarize passed = countif(success == true),
     total = count()
   | project passed
   ",
   log: log
   );
   log.Info($"Executing real-time Power BI run at:
    {DateTime.Now}");
}

private static async Task RealTimeFeedRun( string query,
 TraceWriter log)
{
   log.Info($"Feeding Data to Power BI has started at:
    {DateTime.Now}");
   string requestId = Guid.NewGuid().ToString();
   using (var httpClient = new HttpClient())
   {
      httpClient.DefaultRequestHeaders.Add("x-api-key",
       AiAppKey);
      httpClient.DefaultRequestHeaders.Add("x-ms-app",
       "FunctionTemplate");
      httpClient.DefaultRequestHeaders.Add("x-ms-client-
       request-id", requestId);
      string apiPath = $"{AppInsightsApi}/{AiAppId}/query?
       clientId={requestId}&timespan=P1D&query={query}";
      using (var httpResponse = await
       httpClient.GetAsync(apiPath))
      {
         httpResponse.EnsureSuccessStatusCode();
         var resultJson = await
          httpResponse.Content.ReadAsAsync<JToken>();
         double result;
         if (!double.TryParse(resultJson.SelectToken
           ("Tables[0].Rows[0][0]")?.ToString(), out result))
         {
            throw new FormatException("Query must result in a
             single metric number. Try it on Analytics before
```

```
      scheduling.");
    }
    string postData = $"[{{ \"requests\": \"{result}\"
    }}]";
    log.Verbose($"[Verbose]: Sending data: {postData}");
    using (var response = await
     httpClient.PostAsync(RealTimePushURL, new
     ByteArrayContent(Encoding.UTF8.GetBytes(postData))))
     {
         log.Verbose($"[Verbose]: Data sent with response:
         {response.StatusCode}");
     }
   }
  }
 }
}
```

3. The preceding code runs an AI analytics query that pulls data for the last five minutes (requests) and pushes the data to Power BI push URL. This process repeats continuously based on the timer frequency that you have configured.

4. This is a screenshot that has a sequence of pictures that show the real-time data:

How it works...

We have created the following in the speific order:

- A streaming dataset in the Power BI application
- A dashboard and new tile that can display the values available in the streaming dataset
- A new Azure Function that runs an AI analytics query and feeds data to the Power BI using the push URL of the dataset
- Once everything is done, we can view the real-time data in the Power BI's tile of the dashboard

There's more...

- Power BI allows us to create real-time data in the reports in multiple ways. In this recipe, you learned how to create real-time reports using steaming dataset. The other ways are the Push dataset and the PubNub streaming dataset. You can learn more about all three approaches at `https://powerbi.microsoft.com/en-us/documentation/powerbi-service-real-time-streaming/`.
- Be very careful when you would like to have the real-time application's health data. The AI API has a rate limit. Take a look at `https://dev.applicationinsights.io/documentation/Authorization/Rate-limits` to understand more about API limits.

7
Code Reusability and Refactoring the Code in Azure Functions

In this chapter, you will learn the following recipes:

- Creating a common code repository for better manageability within a function app
- Shared code across Azure Functions using class libraries
- Azure Functions and precompiled assemblies
- Migrating legacy C# application classes to Azure Functions using PowerShell
- Using strongly typed classes in Azure Functions

Introduction

For every business application, there might be some code that is reusable in different modules. So, it's important that your code should reusable to save efforts of your development time. In this chapter, we will learn how to created shared classes and use them in the serverless functions. We will also learn how to migrate the existing background applications into Azure Functions with minimum efforts.

Creating a common code repository for better manageability within a function app

In all our previous chapters, we wrote all the code in the run function. I did that to make everything simple and focus more on conceptual stuff related to Azure Functions instead of code architecture and all. Now, it's time to discuss the features that Azure Functions provide related to code architecture and re-usability. Most of the recipes covered in this chapter talk about them.

In our RegisterUser function, we could refactor the code into multiple classes and functions. However, we will not focus on refactoring all the code, but we will just pull out the code related to sending the emails.

 In your application, make sure you use the architectural design principles and practices based on your requirements.

Let's start refactoring the code.

How to do it...

1. Create a new **ManualTrigger - C#** template, as shown in the following screenshot, with the name SharedClasses:

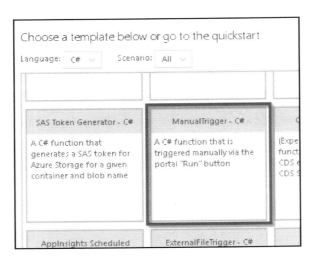

2. Once the trigger is created, navigate to the **View files** tab and add a new file named Helper.csx by clicking on the **Add** button, as shown in the following screenshot:

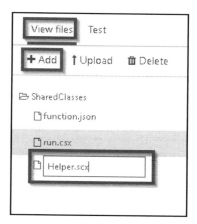

3. Copy the following code and paste in the new Helper.csx file. The following code accepts all the information required for sending an email using SendGrid:

```
#r "SendGrid"
using System.Net;
using SendGrid.Helpers.Mail;
public static class Helper
{
    public static Mail SendMail(string strSubject, string
      strBody,string strFromAddress,string strToAddress,string
      strAttachmentName)
    {
        Mail objMessage = new Mail();
        objMessage.Subject = strSubject;
        objMessage.From = new Email(strFromAddress);

        objMessage.AddContent(new Content("text/html",strBody));

        Personalization personalization = new Personalization();
        personalization.AddTo(new Email(strToAddress));
        objMessage.AddPersonalization(personalization);

        Attachment objAttachment = new Attachment();
        objAttachment.Content = System.Convert.ToBase64String
          (System.Text.Encoding.UTF8.GetBytes(strBody));
        objAttachment.Filename = strAttachmentName;
        objMessage.AddAttachment(objAttachment);
```

```
                    return objMessage;
        }
    }
```

4. Now, let's make the changes to the `Run` method of the `RegisterUser` function that can use the preceding `SendMail` shared method. This is the updated `Run` method that uses the `SendMail` method of `SharedClasses`:

```
#r "Microsoft.WindowsAzure.Storage"
#r "Twilio.Api"
#r "SendGrid"

#load "..\SharedClasses\Helper.csx"

using System.Net;
using SendGrid.Helpers.Mail;
using Microsoft.WindowsAzure.Storage.Table;
using Newtonsoft.Json;
using Twilio;
using Microsoft.Azure.WebJobs.Host.Bindings.Runtime;

public static void Run(HttpRequestMessage req,
                       TraceWriter log,
                       CloudTable objUserProfileTable,
                       out string objUserProfileQueueItem,
                       out Mail message,
                       IBinder binder,
                       out SMSMessage objsmsmessage
                       )
{
    var inputs = req.Content.ReadAsStringAsync().Result;
    dynamic inputJson = JsonConvert.DeserializeObject<dynamic>
      (inputs);
    objUserProfileQueueItem = inputJson.ProfilePicUrl;
    string firstname= inputJson.firstname;
    string lastname=inputJson.lastname;
    string email = inputJson.email;
    string profilePicUrl = inputJson.ProfilePicUrl;
    UserProfile objUserProfile = new UserProfile(firstname,
      lastname,profilePicUrl,email);
    TableOperation objTblOperationInsert = TableOperation.Insert
      (objUserProfile);
    TableResult objTableResult = objUserProfileTable.Execute
      (objTblOperationInsert);
    UserProfile objInsertedUser = (UserProfile)
      objTableResult.Result;
```

```
     string strFromEmailAddress = "donotreply@example.com";
     string strSubject = "New User got registered successfully.";
     string emailContent = "Thank you <b>" + firstname + " " +
      lastname +"</b> for your registration.<br><br>" +
      "Below are the details that you have provided us<br><br>"+
      "<b>First name:</b> " + firstname + "<br>" +
      "<b>Last name:</b> " + lastname + "<br>" +
      "<b>Email Address:</b> " + email + "<br>" +
      "<b>Profile Url:</b> " + profilePicUrl + "<br><br><br>" +
      "Best Regards," + "<br>" + "Website Team";
     string strAttachmentName = firstname + "_" + lastname +
      ".log";

     message = Helper.SendMail(strSubject,emailContent,
      strFromEmailAddress,email,strAttachmentName);

    using (var emailLogBloboutput = binder.Bind<TextWriter>(new
     BlobAttribute($"userregistrationemaillogs/
     {objInsertedUser.RowKey}.log")))
     {
        emailLogBloboutput.WriteLine(emailContent);
     }
    objsmsmessage = new SMSMessage();
    objsmsmessage.Body = "Hello.. Thank you for getting
     registered.";
}
public class UserProfile : TableEntity
{
    public UserProfile(string lastName, string firstName,string
     profilePicUrl,string email)
    {
       this.PartitionKey = "p1";
       this.RowKey = Guid.NewGuid().ToString();;
       this.FirstName = firstName;
       this.LastName = lastName;
       this.ProfilePicUrl = profilePicUrl;
       this.Email = email;
    }
    public UserProfile() { }
    public string FirstName { get; set; }
    public string LastName { get; set; }
    public string ProfilePicUrl {get; set;}
    public string Email { get; set; }
}
```

How it works...

To create shared code and classes, we have taken a **ManualTrigger - C#** template and created a new `.csx` file for our classes (in this case, `Helper`). Once the C# script (`.csx`) files are ready, we can write the common code in those files based on our requirements.

After the shared classes are developed, we can use them in any of the Azure Functions within the function app where these shared classes are located.

To consume the shared classes, we just need to use the `#load` directive to refer to the shared classes using the relative path. In this case, we have used the `#load` `"../SharedClasses/Helper.csx"` directive to refer to the classes located in the `Helper.csx` file located in the `SharedClasses` folder.

There's more...

One of the limitations of these shared classes is that you cannot use the `Helper` class in other Azure Function apps. We will look at how to overcome this limitation in a moment using the class libraries in Visual Studio.

All the changes that you make to these shared classes should be reflected in the caller functions automatically. If, by any chance, if you don't see these changes reflected in the caller functions, navigate to the `host.json` file using **App Service Editor**. Typically, this would happen if your script files are located in other directories.

Navigate to the **App Service Editor**, which is available in **Platform features** under the **DEVELOPMENT TOOLS** sections, as shown in the following screenshot:

Add the `WatchDirectories` attribute to the `host.json` file, as shown in the following screenshot:

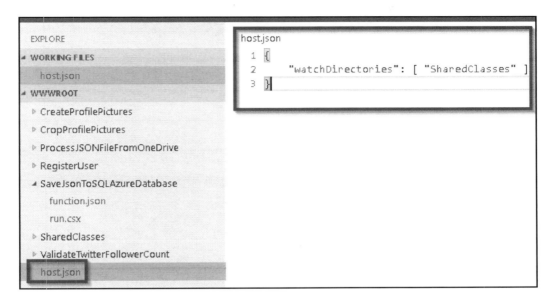

See also

- The *Shared code across Azure Functions using class libraries* recipe

Shared code across Azure Functions using class libraries

You learned how to reuse a `Helper` method within the Azure Function app. However, you cannot reuse the across other function apps or any other type of application such as **Web app**, **WPF Application**, and so on. In this recipe, we will develop and create a new `.dll` file and you will learn how to use the classes and its methods in the Azure Functions.

How to do it...

1. Create a new **Class Library** application using Visual Studio 2015 with **.NET Framework 4.6.1**, as shown in the following screenshot:

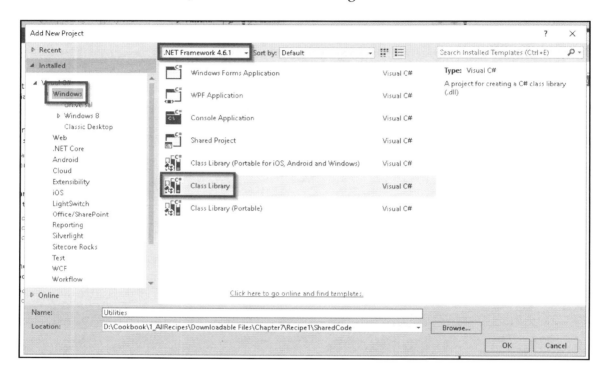

2. Create a new class named `EMailFormatter` and paste the following code in the new class file:

```
namespace Utilities
{
    public static class EMailFormatter
    {
        public static string FrameBodyContent(string firstname,
        string lastname, string email, string profilePicUrl)
        {
            string strBody = "Thank you <b>" + firstname + " " +
            lastname + "</b> for your registration.<br><br>" +
            "Below are the details that you have provided us<br>
            <br>" + "<b>First name:</b> " + firstname + "<br>" +
            "<b>Last name:</b> " + lastname + "<br>" + "<b>Email
```

```
Address:</b> " + email + "<br>" + "<b>Profile Url:
</b> " + profilePicUrl + "<br><br><br>" + "Best
Regards," + "<br>" + "Website Team";
    return strBody;
    }
  }
}
```

3. Change **Build Configuration** to **Release** and build the application to create the `.dll` file, which will be used in our Azure Functions.

4. Navigate to **App Service Editor** of the function app and create a new `bin` folder, by right-clicking in the empty area below the files located in **WWWROOT**, as shown in the following screenshot:

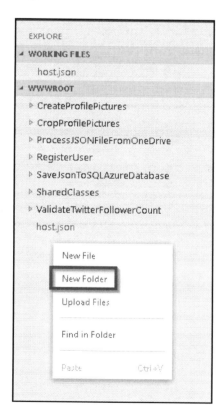

5. After clicking on the **New Folder** item in the preceding screenshot, a new textbox will appear. Provide the name as `bin`, as shown in the following screenshot:

6. After creating the `bin` folder, right-click on the `bin` folder, as shown in the following screenshot, and select `Upload Files` options to upload the `.dll` file that we have created in Visual Studio:

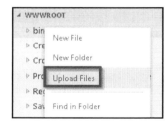

7. This is how it looks after we upload the `.dll` file to the `bin` folder:

8. Navigate to the Azure Function where you would like to use the `shared` method. Let's navigate to the `RegisterUser` function and make the following changes:

   1. Add a new `#r` directive, shown as follows, to the `run.csx` method of the `RegisterUser` Azure Function. Note that `.dll` is required in this case:

   ```
   #r "..\bin\Utilities.dll"
   ```

2. Add a new namespace, shown as follows:

```
using Utilities;
```

9. We are now ready to use the `FrameBodyContent` shared method in our Azure Function. Now replace the existing code that frames the email body content with the following code:

```
string emailContent = EMailFormatter.FrameBodyContent(
    firstname,lastname,email,profilePicUrl);
```

How it works...

1. We have created a `.dll` file that contains the reusable code that can be used in any of the Azure Functions that require the functionality available in the `.dll` file.
2. Once the `.dll` file is ready, we create a `bin` folder in the function app and add the `.dll` file to the `bin` folder.

Note that we have added the `bin` folder to the **WWWROOT** so that it is available to all the Azure Functions available in the function app.

There's more...

Just in case you would like to use the shared code only in one function, then you need to add the `bin` folder along with the `.ddl` file in the required Azure Function folder.

Another major advantage of using class libraries it that it would improve performance as they are already compiled and ready for execution.

See also

The *Creating common code repository for better manageability within a function app* recipe

Azure Functions and precompiled assemblies

In all our Azure Functions that we have created so far, we have written our code in a method named `Run` in the `run.csx`. However, there might be some scenarios where you would like to have your own classes and functions run as a start up method hosted on the Azure Functions. In this recipe, you will learn how to integrate your custom class and methods as start ups.

Getting ready...

By default, all the Function apps that you create in VS 2017 are precompiled function. This recipe is developed using VS 2015. Please make sure you install Visual Studio 2015 if you don't have one installed already.

How to do it...

We need to follow the below steps to create and use the precompiled functions:

1. Create a class library using Visual Studio
2. Create a HTTP function and then make changes to the `Function.json` to integrate the `.ddl` file created in the previous step.

Creating a class library using Visual Studio

1. Create a new **Class Library** named `PrecompiledFunctions` using Visual Studio. Make sure that you choose the latest .NET version framework.
2. Create a new class named `MyFunction` and paste the following code in the new class file. It's nothing new; I just copied the code that gets by default when you create a new HTTP trigger using C# language:

```
using System.Net;
using System.Linq;
using System.Threading.Tasks;
using System.Net.Http;

namespace PreCompiledFunctionSample
{
```

```
public class MyFunction
{
    public static async Task<HttpResponseMessage>
    MyRun(HttpRequestMessage req)
    {
        // parse query parameter
        string name = req.GetQueryNameValuePairs()
         .FirstOrDefault(q => string.Compare(q.Key, "name",
         true) == 0).Value;

        dynamic data = await
         req.Content.ReadAsAsync<object>();
        name = name ?? data?.name;
        return name == null
         ? req.CreateResponse(HttpStatusCode.BadRequest,
         "Please pass a name on the query string or in the
          request body") : req.CreateResponse
          (HttpStatusCode.OK, "Hello " + name);
    }
}
}
```

3. Run the following command in **Package Manager Console**:

```
Install-Package Microsoft.Azure.WebJobs.Extensions -Version 2.0.0
```

4. Run the following command in **Package Manager Console**:

```
Install-Package Microsoft.AspNet.WebApi.Client
```

Creating a new HTTP trigger Azure Function

1. Navigate to your Azure Management portal and create an HTTP trigger Azure Function named `HttpTrigger-MyCompiled` by selecting C# in the language drop-down, as shown here:

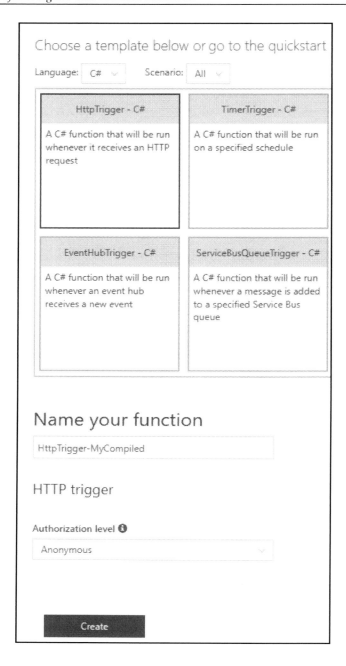

2. Provide a meaningful name and configure **Authorization Level** to **Anonymous**.
3. Delete the default `run.csx` file.
4. Navigate to **App Service Editor** of the function app and go to the `HttpTrigger-MyCompiled` folder, create a folder named `bin`, and upload the `.dll` file along with any other dependencies, if any. In this recipe, we just have the `.ddl` file, as shown in the following screenshot:

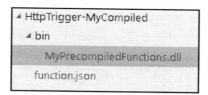

5. Navigate to `function.json` in the Azure Function code editor file and replace the default JSON with the following JSON and save it. Just in case you made changes to your name space, class, or method names, make the changes are according to the following `function.json`:

```
{
    "scriptFile": "bin\\MyPrecompiledFunctions.dll",
    "entryPoint": "PreCompiledFunctionSample.MyFunction.MyRun",
    "bindings": [
    {
        "authLevel": "anonymous",
        "name": "req",
        "type": "httpTrigger",
        "direction": "in"
    },
    {
        "name": "$return",
        "type": "http",
        "direction": "out"
    }
    ],
        "disabled": false
}
```

6. Now, copy the function URL using the **GET** function URL link, which is available just above the code editor and make a request to the HTTP trigger function using the Postman tool:

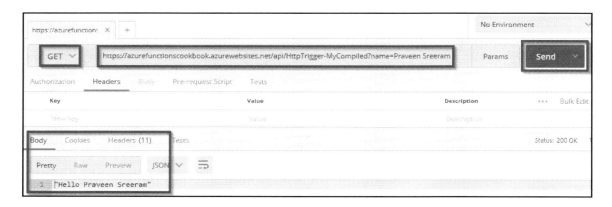

How it works...

These are the steps that we have followed in this recipe:

1. Create a class library using C# with the code that responds to HTTP requests and send an HTTP response.
2. Create an assembly and uploaded it to the Azure Function.
3. To utilize the function named MyRun available in the assembly (.ddl), we need to make the following changes to the Azure Function files:
    1. Delete the default run.csx file.
    2. Add the following to the function.json file:
        - scriptFile: This indicates the location of the .ddl file.
        - entryPoint: This indicates the function name that should be called for every HTTP request to the Azure Function.

There's more...

Even after installing the two NuGet packages mentioned previously, if you get any syntax errors, make sure that you also create a reference to **System.Web.Http** as shown in the following screenshot then click on **OK** button:

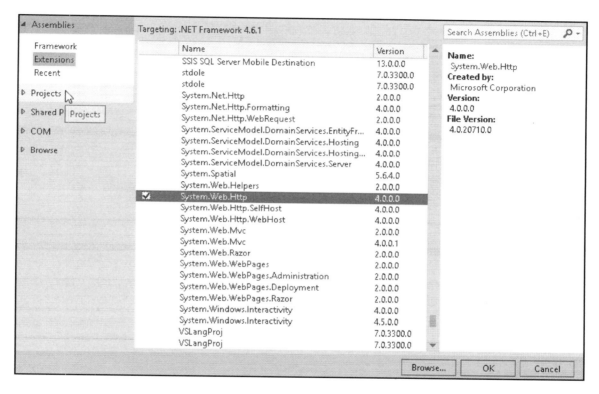

You should have all the following references:

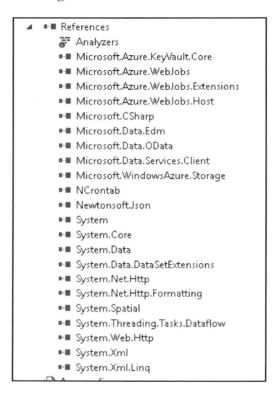

See also

The *Migrating legacy C# application classes to Azure Functions using PowerShell* recipe

Migrating legacy C# application classes to Azure Functions using PowerShell

Currently, many business applications are being hosted in private clouds or on-premise data centers. Many of them have started migrating their applications to Azure using various methods. The following are a just a few methods of quick migration to Azure:

- **Lift and shift the legacy application to the Infrastructure as a service (IaaS) environment**: This method should be straight forward, as you have complete control over the virtual machines that you would create. You could host all your web applications, schedulers, databases, and so on without making any changes to your application code. You can even install any third-party software's or libraries. Though this option provides full control for your application, it would be expensive in most of the cases as the background application might not be running all the time.

- **Convert legacy applications to Platform as a service (PaaS)-compatible environment**: This method could be complex depending on how many dependencies your applications have in other third-party libraries that are not compatible with the Azure PaaS environment. You would need to make code changes to your applications so that they are stateless and are not dependent on any of the resources of the instances where they are hosted. This option is very cost-effective as you just need to pay for the execution time of your applications.

In order to host your applications in Azure and utilize them to fullest possible extent, your applications shouldn't be dependent on any of the resources of the virtual machine instances on which they would be hosted. For example, you should use **Redis Cache** to store all your user session information instead of using In-Proc sessions.

In this recipe, we will look at one of the easiest ways of migrating your existing background job applications developed using C# classes and console applications without making many changes to the existing application code.

We will be using a timer trigger to run the job every 5 minutes. And we will use PowerShell to invoke the `.exe` process of the console application.

Getting ready

It is recommended that you install Visual Studio 2015 if you don't have one installed already.

How to do it...

We will perform this recipe using the following steps:

Creating an application using Visual Studio

1. Create a new console application and name it BackgroundJob using Visual Studio. Make sure that you choose the latest .NET version framework.

2. Create a new class called UserRegistration and replace the following code:

```
using System;
namespace BackgroundJob
{
    class UserRegistration
    {
        public static void RegisterUser()
        {
            Console.WriteLine("Register User method of
              UserRegistration has been called.");
        }
    }
}
```

3. Create a new class called OrderProcessing and replace the following code:

```
using System;
namespace BackgroundJob
{
    class OrderProcessing
    {
        public static void ProcessOrder()
        {
            Console.WriteLine("Process Order method of
              OrderProcessing class has been called");
        }
    }
}
```

4. In the `Program.cs` file, replace the existing code with the following code:

```
using System;
namespace BackgroundJob
{
    class Program
    {
        static void Main(string[] args)
        {
         Console.WriteLine("Main method execution has been
           started");
         Console.WriteLine
           ("======================================");
         UserRegistration.RegisterUser();
         OrderProcessing.ProcessOrder();
         Console.WriteLine
           ("======================================");
         Console.WriteLine("Main method execution has been
           completed");
        }
    }
}
```

5. Build the application to create the `.exe` file. You can configure it to run in either debug or release mode. It is recommended that you deploy `.exe` in the release mode in your production environments.

Creating a new PowerShell Azure Function

1. Navigate to your Azure Management portal and create a **TimerTrigger - PowerShell** Azure Function by selecting **PowerShell** in the **Language** dropdown, as shown in the following screenshot:

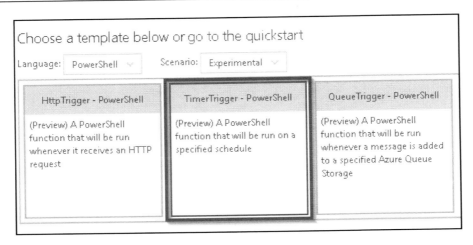

2. Provide a meaningful name and configure the function to run every 5 minutes by setting the frequency in the **Schedule** field, as shown in the following screenshot:

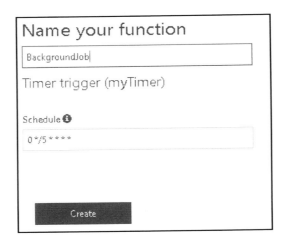

3. Navigate to **App Service Editor** of the function app and go to the BackgroundJob folder, create a folder named bin, and upload the .exe file along with any other dependencies if any. In this recipe, we have just the .exe file, as shown in the following screenshot:

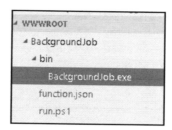

4. Once you have uploaded the .exe file, you can also view it in the **View Files** section of the Azure Function, as shown in the following screenshot. You can view the .exe file by clicking on the **bin** folder icon:

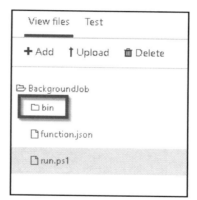

5. Navigate to the run.ps1 file and replace the default code with the following code and save it:

```
& "D:\home\site\wwwroot\BackgroundJob\bin\BackgroundJob.exe"
```

6. Click on the **Run** button to run a test to check whether it's working as expected. In my case, clicking on the **Run** button has created the following log, which is expected:

```
2017-07-06T11:35:02.061 Function started (Id=6b29bde6-145a-400c-bdc4-19429948f48c)
2017-07-06T11:35:03.156 Main method execution has been started
2017-07-06T11:35:03.156 ======================================
2017-07-06T11:35:03.156 Register User method of UserRegistration has been called.
2017-07-06T11:35:03.156 Process Order method of OrderProcessing class has been called
2017-07-06T11:35:03.156 ======================================
2017-07-06T11:35:03.156 Main method execution has been completed
2017-07-06T11:35:03.171 Function completed (Success, Id=6b29bde6-145a-400c-bdc4-19429948f4
```

How it works...

In this recipe, we have created a simple application that has a single function in each of the two classes that just print the message when it is called. Once the development of the classes is complete, you can learn how to create a new Azure Function and integrate it with the `.exe` file. In your real-work cases, you can also upload your `.exe` files along with any other libraries to the Azure Function app folder and use them for your needs.

See also

- The *Azure Functions and precompiled assemblies* recipe
- The *Shared code across Azure Functions using class libraries* recipe

Using strongly typed classes in Azure Functions

In our initial chapters, we developed an HTTP trigger named `RegisterUser` that acts as a Web API that could be consumed by any application that's capable of making HTTP requests. However, there might be some other requirements where you might have different applications that create messages in a queue with the details required for creating a user. For the sake of simplicity, we will be using Azure Storage Explorer to create a queue message.

In this recipe, we will look at how to get the details of the user from the queue using strongly typed objects.

Getting ready

Before moving further perform the following steps:

1. Create a storage account named `azurefunctionscookbook` in your Azure subscription.
2. Install Microsoft Azure Storage Explorer if you haven't installed it already.
3. Once storage explorer is created, connect to your Azure storage account.

How to do it...

1. Using the Azure Storage Explorer, create a queue named `registeruserqueue` in the storage account named `azurefunctionscookbook`. We assume that all the other applications would be creating messages in the `registeruserqueue` queue.
2. Navigate to Azure Functions and create a new Azure Function using **QueueTrigger - C#** and choose the queue that we have created, as shown in the following screenshot:

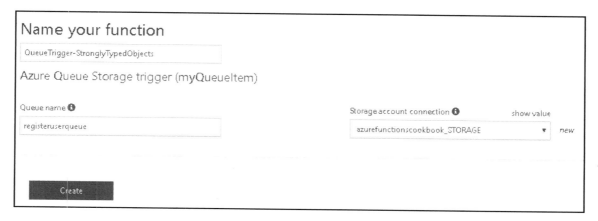

3. Replace the default code with the following code:

```
using System;
public static void Run(User myQueueItem, TraceWriter log)
{
    log.Info($"A Message has been created for a new User");
    log.Info($"First name: {myQueueItem.firstname}" );
    log.Info($"Last name: {myQueueItem.lastname}" );
    log.Info($"email: {myQueueItem.email}" );
    log.Info($"Profile Pic Url: {myQueueItem.ProfilePicUrl}" );
}
public class User
{
    public string firstname { get;set;}
    public string lastname { get;set;}
    public string email { get;set;}
    public string ProfilePicUrl { get;set;}
}
```

4. Navigate to **Azure Storage Explorer** and create a new message in
    `registeruserqueue,` as shown in the following screenshot:

5. Click on OK to create the queue message and navigate back to the Azure Function and look at the logs, as shown in the following screenshot:

```
Logs                                                    ⏸ Pause  🖫 Clear  📋 Copy logs  ✎ Collapse  ⌄
2017-07-08T09:08:13.868 Function started (Id=95e34cd7-fd6e-4127-a8bf-43b798d0c335)
2017-07-08T09:08:13.884 A Message has been created for a new User
2017-07-08T09:08:13.884 First name: Praveen
2017-07-08T09:08:13.884 Last name: Sreeram
2017-07-08T09:08:13.884 email: prawin2k@gmail.com
2017-07-08T09:08:13.884 Profile Pic Url: https://upload.wikimedia.org/wikipedia/commons/thumb/1/19/Bill_Gates_June_2015.jpg/220px-Bil
2017-07-08T09:08:13.884 Function completed (Success, Id=95e34cd7-fd6e-4127-a8bf-43b798d0c335, Duration=18ms)
```

How it works...

We have developed a new Azure queue function that gets triggered when a new message gets added to the queue. We have created a new queue message with all the details required to create the user. You can further reuse the Azure Function code to pass the user object (in this case, myQueueItem) to the database layer class that is capable of inserting the data into database or any other persistent medium.

There's more...

In this recipe, the type of the queue message parameter that is accepted by the Run method is User. The Azure Function runtime will take care of serializing the JSON message available in the queue to the custom type, User in our case. If you would like to reuse the User class, you can create a new user.csx file and refer to the class in any other Azure Function using the #load directive.

See also

- The *Creating a common code repository for better manageability within a function app* recipe

8

Developing Reliable and Durable Serverless Applications Using Durable Functions

In this chapter, you will learn the following:

- Configuring Durable Functions in the Azure Management portal
- Creating a hello world Durable Function app
- Testing and troubleshooting Durable Functions
- Implementing multithreaded reliable applications using Durable Functions

Please note that the Durable Functions runtime is still in Alpha Preview. Microsoft Azure Function team is working on providing more features. In case you face any issues, please feel free to report the issue here: `https://github.com/Azure/azure-webjobs-sdk-script/issues/`.

Introduction

When you are working on developing modern applications that need to be hosted on the cloud, you need to make sure that the applications are stateless. Statelessness is an essential factor for developing the cloud-aware applications. For example, you should avoid persisting any data in the resource that is specific to any **virtual machine** (**VM**) instance which is provisioned to any Azure Service (for example: App Service, API and so on). If you do so, you cannot leverage few of the services such as the auto scaling functionality as the provisioning of instances is dynamic. If you depend on any VM specific resources, you will end up facing troubles with unexpected behaviors.

Having said that, the downside of the previously mentioned approach is that you end up working on identifying ways of persisting data in different mediums depending on your application architecture.

Azure has come up with a new way of handing statefulness in serverless architecture along with other features such as durability and reliability in the form of Durable Functions. Durable Functions is an extension to Azure Functions and it is in the very early stages of development. By the time you will be reading this, there might be a lot of changes released to the Durable Functions. Please do keep checking the official documentation available in GitHub at `https://azure.github.io/azure-functions-durable-extension/articles/overview.html`.

Configuring Durable Functions in the Azure Management portal

Currently, there are no predefined templates available for creating Durable Functions. Hopefully by the time you are reading this chapter, the Azure Management portal will have the ability to create Durable Functions using the default function templates. If you find any template on the portal for creating the Durable Functions, please feel free to skip this recipe.

Getting ready

Create a new function app named `MyDurableFunction`.

How to do it...

1. Download the Durable Function extension from `https://azure.github.io/azure-functions-durable-extension/articles/overview.html`. It has all the libraries related to the Durable Functions extension.

 Currently, you need to configure these libraries manually. In the near future, Microsoft is planning to release a NuGet Package for a smooth installation experience.

2. Click on the **Advanced tools (Kudu)** link available in the **Platform Settings** tab under **Development Tools** section of your function app.

3. In the **Kudu** console, click on **CMD** as shown in the following screenshot:

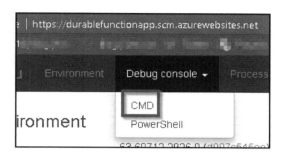

4. As shown in the following screenshot, click on the + icon and then select **New folder** to create a new folder:

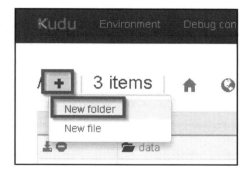

5. After clicking on the **New folder** menu item, a new text-box will appear for you to enter the name of the folder. Please provide the name as `BindingExtensions`. Once the `BindingExtension` folder is created, click on it to navigate to its contents. As it is a new folder, it would be empty. Let's drag and drop the `DurableTask` folder from your local machine to the `BindingExtensions` folder on **Kudu** console. Once the upload process is done, your **Kudu** console's view should be something similar to as shown in the following screenshot:

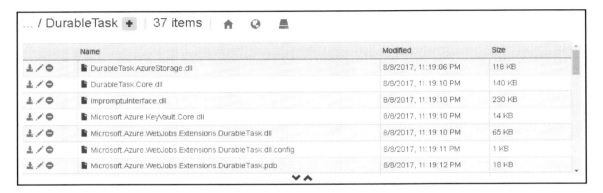

Though all major browsers should support drag and drop functionality. It is recommended to use Google Chrome for better experience of the drag and drop feature especially when you drag and drop the entire `.zip` file.

6. Within the preceding step, scroll down a bit to see the command view of the folder where you can see the complete physical path of the folder within the VM allocated for the function app. It should be in the following path: `D:\home\BindingExtensions\DurableTask`.

7. We need to let the runtime know the path of the Durable Function libraries using the **Application settings**. Let's configure it by navigating to the **Application Setting** under **GENERAL SETTINGS** of the **Platform features** tab as shown in the following screenshot:

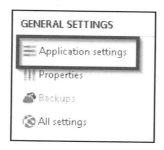

8. In **Application settings,** create a new key
   named AzureWebJobs_ExtensionsPath with the
   value D:\home\BindingExtensions (please exclude the DurableTask folder
   name from the value) and click on the **Save** button to save the changes as shown
   in the following screenshot:

Please also notice that at the time of writing this book, there was a problem with the latest version (~1) of the Azure Function framework. So I had to rely on one of the stable versions which is highlighted in the preceding screenshot.

There's more...

Durable Functions is still in the Alpha stage and it is not recommended to be used in your production environment.

See also

- The *Creating a hello world Durable Function app* recipe
- The *Configuring Durable Functions in the Azure Management portal* recipe
- The *Testing and troubleshooting Durable Functions* recipe

Creating a hello world Durable Function app

Though the overall intention of this book is to have each recipe of every chapter solve at least one business problem, this recipe however, doesn't solve any real-time domain problems, but it provides a quick start guidance to the readers to understand more about Durable Functions and its components along with the approach of developing Durable Functions.

Developing and testing the Durable Functions is not straightforward at this point of time. Hopefully, the next set of recipes will help you to start exploring all the features of Durable Functions.

Getting ready

We will perform the following steps before moving ahead:

- Please install Postman tool from `https://www.getpostman.com/` if you haven't installed it yet.
- Please read more about Orchestrator and Activity trigger bindings at `https://azure.github.io/azure-functions-durable-extension/articles/topics/bindings.html`

How to do it...

In order to develop Durable Functions, we need to create the following three functions:

- **Orchestrator client**: An Azure Function that can manage the Orchestrator instances
- **Orchestrator function**: The actual Orchestrator function allows the development stateful workflows via code and can asynchronously call other Azure Functions (which are called as **Activity functions**) and can even save the return values of those functions into local variables
- **Activity functions**: These are the functions which will be called by the Orchestrator functions

Creating HttpStart Function - the Orchestrator client

1. Create a new HTTP function named `HttpStart` with **Authorization Level** as **Anonymous** in the `DurableFunctionApp` function app:

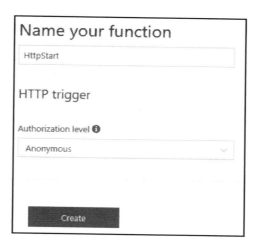

2. Immediately after creating the function, you will be taken to the code editor. Please replace the default code with the following code and click on the **Save** button to save the changes:

```
#r "Microsoft.Azure.WebJobs.Extensions.DurableTask"
#r "Newtonsoft.Json"
using System.Net;
public static async Task<HttpResponseMessage> Run(
```

```
HttpRequestMessage req,
DurableOrchestrationClient initiator,
string functionName,
TraceWriter log)
{
   dynamic eventData = await req.Content.ReadAsAsync<object>();
   string instanceId = await
    initiator.StartNewAsync(functionName,
    eventData);

   log.Info($"Started orchestration with ID =
    '{instanceId}'.");

   return initiator.CreateCheckStatusResponse(req, instanceId);
}
```

3. Navigate to the **Integrate** tab and click on **Advanced editor** as shown in the following screenshot:

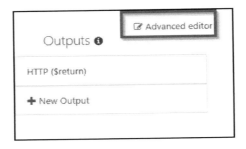

4. In the **Advanced editor**, replace the default code with the following code:

```
{
    "bindings": [
    {
        "authLevel": "anonymous",
        "name": "req",
        "type": "httpTrigger",
        "direction": "in",
        "route": "orchestrators/{functionName}",
        "methods": [
        "post"
                ]
    },
    {
        "name": "$return",
        "type": "http",
        "direction": "out"
```

```
    },
    {
        "name": "initiator",
        "type": "orchestrationClient",
        "direction": "in"
    }
    ],
        "disabled": false
}
```

The HttpStart function works like a gateway for invoking all the functions in the function app. Any request you make using the https://mydurablefunction.azurewebsites.net/api/orchest rators/{functionName} format in the URL, will be received by this HttpStart function and it will take care of executing the Orchestrator function based on the parameter available in the route parameter {functionName}. All this is possible with the route attribute in the function.json of the HttpStart function.

Creating Orchestrator function

1. Create a new function named DurableFuncManager using the **ManualTrigger-C#**, replace the default code with the following code and click on the **Save** button to save the changes:

```
#r "Microsoft.Azure.WebJobs.Extensions.DurableTask"
public static async Task<List<string>>
 Run(DurableOrchestrationContext context)
{
    var outputs = new List<string>();
    outputs.Add(await context.CallFunctionAsync<string>
     ("ConveyGreeting", "Welcome Cookbook Readers"));
    return outputs;
}
```

2. In the **Advanced editor** of the **Integrate** tab, replace the default code with the following code:

```
{
    "bindings": [
    {
        "name": "context",
        "type": "orchestrationTrigger",
        "direction": "in"
```

```
    }
  ],
  "disabled": false
}
```

Creating Activity function

1. Create a new function named `ConveyGreeting` using the **ManualTrigger-C#**, replace the default code with the following code and click on the **Save** button to save the changes:

```
#r "Microsoft.Azure.WebJobs.Extensions.DurableTask"
public static string Run(DurableActivityContext
 greetingContext)
{
    string name = greetingContext.GetInput<string>();
    return $"Hello {name}!";
}
```

2. In the **Advanced editor** of the **Integrate** tab, replace the default code with the following code:

```
{
    "bindings": [
    {
       "name": "greetingContext",
       "type": "activityTrigger",
       "direction": "in"
    }
    ],
  "disabled": false
}
```

In this recipe, we have created an Orchestration client, an Orchestrator function, and Activity function. We will learn how to test these in our next recipe.

How it works...

Let us take a look at the working of the recipe:

- We first developed the Orchestrator client (in our case it is `HttpStart`) which is capable of creating the Orchestrators using the `StartNewAsync` function of the `DurableOrchestrationClient` class. This method creates a new Orchestrator instance.
- Secondly, we developed the Orchestrator Function which is the most crucial piece of the Durable Functions. Following are few of the important core features of the Orchestrator context:
    - It can invoke multiple Activity functions
    - It can save the output returned by an Activity function (say `ActFun1`) and pass it to another Activity function (say `ActFun2`)
    - These Orchestrator functions are also capable of creating checkpoints which saves the execution points so that in case if there is any problem with the VMs then it can replace/resume automatically
- And lastly, we developed the Activity function where we write most of the business logic. In our case, it's just returning a simple message.

There's more...

- Currently, there is no function template support for Durable Functions. So we have created Manual triggers and updated the bindings using JSON code. Microsoft Azure team might come up with the required templates for Durable Functions very soon.

See also

- The *Configuring Durable Functions in the Azure Management portal* recipe
- The *Testing and troubleshooting Durable Functions* recipe
- The *Implementing multithreaded reliable application using Durable Functions* recipe

Testing and troubleshooting Durable Functions

In all our previous chapters, we have discussed various ways of testing the Azure Functions. We can test the Durable Functions with the same set of tools. However the testing approach is entirely different because of its features and the way it works.

In this recipe, we will learn few of the essential things that one should be aware of while working with Durable Functions.

Getting ready

Please install the following if you haven't installed them yet:

- Postman tool from `https://www.getpostman.com/`
- Azure Storage Explorer from `http://storageexplorer.com/`

How to do it...

1. Navigate to the code editor of the `HttpStart` function and grab the URL by clicking on the **</>Get function URL** and replace the `{functionName}` template value with `DurableFuncManager`.
2. Let's make a `POST` request using Postman as shown in the following screenshot:

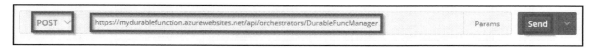

3. Once you click on the **Send** button you will get a response with the following:
   - Instance ID
   - URL for retrieving the status of the function
   - URL to send an event to the function
   - URL to terminate the request

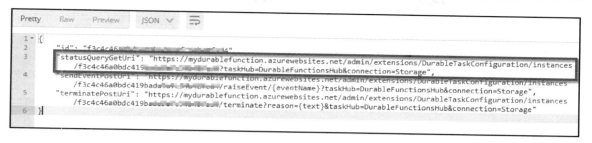

4. Click on the `statusQueryGetURi` in the preceding step to view the status of the function. Clicking on the link in the preceding step will open it in a new tab within the Postman tool. Once the new tab is opened, click on the **Send** button to get the actual output:

```
{
    "runtimeStatus": "Completed",
    "input": null,
    "output": [
        "Hello Welcome Cookbook Readers!"
    ],
    "createdTime": "2017-08-10T04:43:15Z",
    "lastUpdatedTime": "2017-08-10T04:43:33Z"
}
```

5. If everything goes well (as in my case) we can see the `runtimeStatus` as `Completed` as shown in the preceding screenshot within the postman, you will also get eight records in the Table storage where the execution history is stored as shown in the following screenshot:

EventType	ExecutionId
OrchestratorStarted	a426ec4dabe44527a6aeae14290802c1
ExecutionStarted	a426ec4dabe44527a6aeae14290802c1
TaskScheduled	a426ec4dabe44527a6aeae14290802c1
OrchestratorCompleted	a426ec4dabe44527a6aeae14290802c1
OrchestratorStarted	a426ec4dabe44527a6aeae14290802c1
TaskCompleted	a426ec4dabe44527a6aeae14290802c1
ExecutionCompleted	a426ec4dabe44527a6aeae14290802c1
OrchestratorCompleted	a426ec4dabe44527a6aeae14290802c1

6. If something has gone wrong, you can see the error message in the result column which tells you in which function the error has occurred, and then you need to navigate to the **Monitor** tab of that function to see a detailed error of the same.

See also

- The *Creating a hello world Durable Function app* recipe
- The *Configuring Durable Functions in the Azure Management portal* recipe
- The *Implementing multithreaded reliable application using Durable Functions* recipe

Implementing multithreaded reliable applications using Durable Functions

I have worked in few of the applications where parallel execution is required to perform some computing tasks. The main advantage of this approach is that you get the desired output pretty quickly depending on the subthreads that you create. It could be achieved in multiple ways using different technologies. However the challenge in these approaches is that if something goes wrong in the middle of any of the subthread it's not easy to self-heal and resume from where it was stopped. I'm sure many of you might have faced similar problems in your application as it is a very common business case.

In this recipe, we will try to implement a simple way of executing a function in parallel with multiple instances using the Durable Functions for the following scenario.

Assume that we have five customers (whose IDs are 1,2,3,4,5) who approached us to generate huge number of barcodes (say around 50 thousand). It would take lot of time for generating the barcodes as it would involve some image processing tasks. So one simple way to quickly process the request is to use asynchronous programming by creating a thread for each of the customer and executing the logic in parallel for each of them.

We will also simulate a simple use case to understand how the Durable Functions auto-heal when the VM in which it is hosted would go down or restart.

Getting ready

Please install the following if you haven't installed them yet:

- Postman tool from `https://www.getpostman.com/`
- Azure Storage Explorer from `http://storageexplorer.com/`

How to do it...

In this recipe, we will create the following Azure Function triggers:

- One Orchestrator function named `GenerateQRCode`
- Two Activity trigger functions:
  - `GetAllCustomers`: This function just returns the array of customer IDs. In your application, you would need to write your business logic.
  - `CreateQRCodeImagesPerCustomer`: This function doesn't actually create the barcode, however it just logs a message to the console as our goal is to understand the features of Durable Functions. For each customer, we will randomly generate a number less than 50,000 and just iterate through it.

Creating Orchestrator function

1. Create a new Function named `GenerateQRCode` using the **ManualTrigger-C#**, replace the default code with the following code and click on the **Save** button to save the changes:

```
#r "Microsoft.Azure.WebJobs.Extensions.DurableTask"

public static async Task<int> Run(DurableOrchestrationContext
  qrCodeContext)
{
    int[] customers = await
     qrCodeContext.CallFunctionAsync<int[]>("GetAllCustomers");

    var tasks = new Task<long>[customers.Length];
    for (int nCustomerIndex = 0; nCustomerIndex <
     customers.Length; nCustomerIndex++)
    {
```

```
        tasks[nCustomerIndex] =
         qrCodeContext.CallFunctionAsync<int>
         ("CreateQRCodeImagesPerCustomer",
         customers[nCustomerIndex]);
    }
    await Task.WhenAll(tasks);
    int nTotalItems = tasks.Sum(item => item.Result);
    return nTotalItems;
}
```

2. In the **Advanced editor** of the **Integrate** tab, replace the default code with the following code:

```
{
    "bindings": [
    {
       "name": "qrCodeContext",
       "type": "orchestrationTrigger",
       "direction": "in"
    }
    ],
    "disabled": false
}
```

Creating Activity function GetAllCustomers

1. Create a new Function named GetAllCustomers using the **ManualTrigger-C#**, replace the default code with the following code and click on the **Save** button to save the changes:

```
#r "Microsoft.Azure.WebJobs.Extensions.DurableTask"
public static int[] Run(DurableActivityContext
 getAllCustomersContext)
{
    int[] customers = new int[]{1,2,3,4,5};
    return customers;
}
```

2. In the **Advanced editor** of the **Integrate** tab, replace the default code with the following code:

```
{
    "bindings": [
    {
        "name": "getAllCustomersContext",
        "type": "activityTrigger",
        "direction": "in"
    }
    ],
    "disabled": false
}
```

Creating Activity function
CreateQRCodeImagesPerCustomer

1. Create a new Function named CreateQRCodeImagesPerCustomer using the
ManualTrigger-C#, replace the default code with the following code and click on
the **Save** button to save the changes:

```
#r "Microsoft.Azure.WebJobs.Extensions.DurableTask"
#r "Microsoft.WindowsAzure.Storage"
using Microsoft.WindowsAzure.Storage.Blob;

public static async Task<int> Run(DurableActivityContext
  customerContext,TraceWriter log)
{
    int ncustomerId = Convert.ToInt32
      (customerContext.GetInput<string>());
    Random objRandom = new Random(Guid.NewGuid().GetHashCode());
    int nRandomValue = objRandom.Next(50000);
    for(int nProcessIndex = 0;nProcessIndex<=nRandomValue;
     nProcessIndex++)
    {
        log.Info($" running for {nProcessIndex}");
    }
    return nRandomValue;
}
```

2. In the **Advanced editor** of the **Integrate** tab, replace the default code with the following code:

```
{
    "bindings": [
    {
        "name": "customerContext",
        "type": "activityTrigger",
        "direction": "in"
    }
    ],
    "disabled": false
}
```

3. Let's run the function using Postman. We will be stopping the App Service (to simulate a restart of the VM where the function would be running and see how the Durable Function resumes from where it was paused).

4. Make a `POST` request using Postman as shown in the following screenshot:

5. Once you click on the **Send** button, you will get a response with the status URL. Click on the `statusQueryGetURi` to view the status of the Function. Clicking on the `statusQueryGetURi` link will open it in a new tab within the Postman tool. Once the new tab is opened, click on the **Send** button to get the progress of the Function.

6. Let's quickly navigate to the Function app's **Overview** tab (while the function is running) and stop the service by clicking on the **Stop** button as shown in the following screenshot:

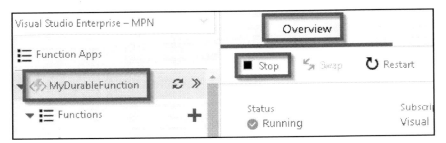

7. The execution of the function will be stopped in the middle. Let's navigate to the storage account to see how much progress has been made as shown in the following screenshot:

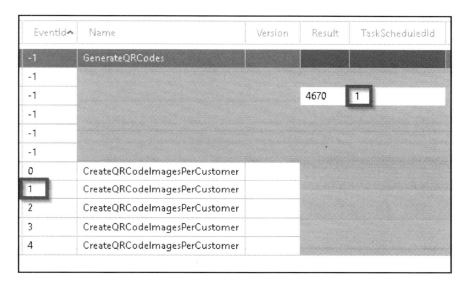

EventId▲	Name	Version	Result	TaskScheduledId
-1	GenerateQRCodes			
-1				
-1			4670	1
-1				
-1				
-1				
0	CreateQRCodeImagesPerCustomer			
1	CreateQRCodeImagesPerCustomer			
2	CreateQRCodeImagesPerCustomer			
3	CreateQRCodeImagesPerCustomer			
4	CreateQRCodeImagesPerCustomer			

8. Let's now go back to the App Service and resume the service. You will notice that the service will resume from where it had stopped. We didn't write any code for this, it's an out-of-the-box feature.

How it works...

Durable Function allows us to develop reliable execution of the functions which means that even if the VMs are restarted or crashed while the function is running, it automatically resumes back to its previous state automatically. It does so with the help of something called as **Checkpointing** and **Replaying,** where the history of the execution is stored in the Storage Table. You can learn more about this feature at https://azure.github.io/azure-functions-durable-extension/articles/topics/checkpointing-and-replay.html.

There's more...

In order to view the Execution history of your Durable Functions, please navigate to the table named `DurableFunctionsHubHistory` which is located in the the Storage Account which is created while creating the Function app, you can find the Storage Account name in the **Application settings** as shown in the following screenshot:

WEBSITE_CONTENTSHARE	mydurablefunction8c72

See also

- The *Creating a hello world Durable function app* recipe
- The *Configuring Durable Functions in the Azure Management portal* recipe
- The *Testing and troubleshooting Durable Functions* recipe

9
Implement Best Practices for Azure Functions

In this chapter, you will learn a few of the best practices that can be followed while working with the Azure Functions such as:

- Adding multiple messages to a Queue using the `IAsyncCollector` function
- Implementing defensive applications using Azure Functions and Queue triggers
- Handling massive ingress using Event Hub for IoT and alike scenarios.
- Enabling authorization for function apps
- Controlling access to Azure Functions using function keys

Adding multiple messages to a Queue using the IAsyncCollector function

In the first chapter, you learned how to create a Queue message for each request coming from the HTTP request. Now let's assume that each user is registering their devices (mobiles, laptops, and so on) using any client application (for example, a desktop app, a mobile app, or any client website) that can send multiple records in a single request. In these cases, the backend application should be smart enough to handle the load coming to it. In these cases, there should be a mechanism to create multiple Queue message in a single go asynchronously. You will learn how to create multiple Queue messages using the `IAsyncCollector` interface.

Here is a sample diagram that depicts the data flow from different client applications to the backend web API:

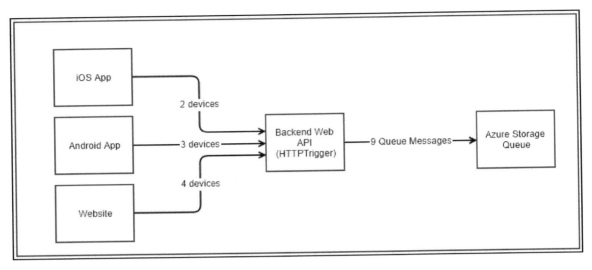

In this recipe, we will simulate the requests using the Postman tool that sends the request to the **Backend Web API (HttpTrigger)** that can create all the Queue messages in a single go.

Getting ready

These are the required steps:

- Create a storage account using Azure Management portal if you have not created it yet.
- Install Microsoft Storage Explorer from `http://storageexplorer.com/` if you have not installed it yet.

How to do it...

1. Create a new HTTP trigger named `BulkDeviceRegistrations` by setting the **Authorization Level** to **Anonymous**.

2. Replace the default code with the following code. You might get compilation errors. Don't worry, we will fix that in the next few steps:

```
using System.Net;
using Newtonsoft.Json;
public static void Run(HttpRequestMessage req, TraceWriter log,
  IAsyncCollector<string>DeviceQueue)
{
    var data = req.Content.ReadAsStringAsync().Result;
    dynamic inputJson = JsonConvert.DeserializeObject<dynamic>
     (data);
    for(int nIndex=0;nIndex<inputJson.devices.Count;nIndex++)
    {
       DeviceQueue.AddAsync
        (Convert.ToString(inputJson.devices
        [nIndex]));
    }
}
```

3. Click on the **Save** button and navigate to the **Integrate** tab and add a new **Azure Queue Storage output** binding then click on **Select** button and provide the name of the Queue and other parameters, as shown in the following screenshot:

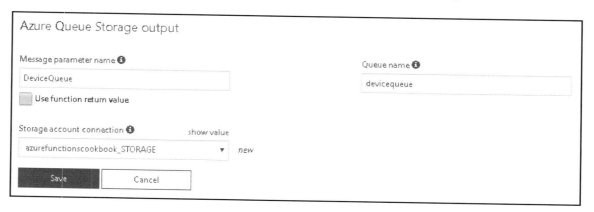

4. Click on the **Save** button to save the changes and navigate to the code editor of the Azure Function.

5. In the code editor, click on the **Viewfiles** tab and add a new file named the `project.json`.

6. Let's add a `Newtonsoft.Json` NuGet package by adding the following JSON in the `project.json` file:

```
{
  "frameworks" : {
          "net46": {
              "dependencies":{
                  "Newtonsoft.Json" : "10.0.2"
                              }
                  }
          }
}
```

7. Let's run the function from the **Test** tab of the portal with the following input request JSON:

```
{
"devices":
    [
       {
         "type": "laptop",
         "brand":"lenovo",
         "model":"T440"
       },
       {
          "type": "mobile",
          "brand":"Mi",
          "model":"Red Mi 4"
       }
    ]
}
```

8. Click on the **Run** button to test the functionality. Now open the Azure Storage Explorer and navigate to the Queue named as `devicequeue`. As shown in the following figure, you should see two records:

How it works...

Create a new HTTP function that has a parameter of type `IAsyncCollector<string>`, which could be used to store multiple messages in a Queue service in a single go asynchronously. This approach of storing multiple items asynchronously will reduce lots of load on the instances. We also added the `Newtonsoft.Json` NuGet package by adding the references in the `project.json` file.

Finally, we ran a test on invoking Http trigger right from the Azure Management portal and also saw the Queue messages get added using the Azure Storage Explorer.

There's more...

You can also use the `ICollector` interface in place of `IAsyncCollector` if you would like to store multiple messages synchronously.

Implementing defensive applications using Azure Functions and Queue triggers

For many of the applications, even after performing multiple tests of different environments, there might still be unforeseen reasons why the application would fail. Developers and architects cannot predict all the unexpected inputs throughout the lifespan of the application being used by the business users or the end users. So, it's a good practice to make sure that your application alerts you and send notifications in case of any errors or unexpected issues with the applications.

In this recipe, you will learn how the Azure Functions help us in handling these kinds of issues with minimal code.

Getting ready

These are the required steps:

- Create a storage account using Azure Management portal if you have not created it yet.
- Install Microsoft storage Explorer from `http://storageexplorer.com/` if you have not installed it yet.

How to do it...

In this recipe, we will develop the following pieces of code:

1. Develop a Console Application using C# that connects to the storage account and creates Queue messages in the Queue named `myqueuemessages`.
2. Create a Azure Function Queue trigger named `ProcessData` that gets fired whenever a new message is being added to the Queue named `myqueuemessages`.

CreateQueueMessage - C# Console Application

1. Create a new Console Application using the C# language. Make sure that you choose the latest framework.

2. Install the `WindowsAzure.Storage` NuGet package using the following command:

   ```
   Install-Package Windowsazure.Storage
   ```

3. Add the following namespaces and a reference to the `System.Configuration.dll` file:

   ```
   using Microsoft.WindowsAzure.Storage;
   using Microsoft.WindowsAzure.Storage.Queue;
   using System.Configuration;
   ```

4. Add the following function to your Console Application and call it from the `Main` method. The `CreateQueueMessages` function creates `100` messages with the index as the content of each message:

   ```
   static void CreateQueueMessages()
   {
       CloudStorageAccount storageAccount =
        CloudStorageAccount.Parse(ConfigurationManager.AppSettings
        ["StorageConnectionString"]);
       CloudQueueClient queueclient =
        storageAccount.CreateCloudQueueClient();

       CloudQueue queue = queueclient.GetQueueReference
        ("myqueuemessages");
       queue.CreateIfNotExists();

       CloudQueueMessage message = null;
       for(int nQueueMessageIndex = 0; nQueueMessageIndex <= 100;
        nQueueMessageIndex++)
       {
           message = new CloudQueueMessage(Convert.ToString
            (nQueueMessageIndex));
           queue.AddMessage(message);
           Console.WriteLine(nQueueMessageIndex);
       }
   }
   ```

Developing the Azure Function - Queue trigger

1. Create a new Azure Function named `ProcessData` using the Queue trigger that monitors the trigger named `myqueuemessages`. This is how the **Integrate** tab should look after you create the function:

2. Replace the default code with the following code:

```
using System;
public static void Run(string myQueueItem,
 TraceWriter log)
{
    if(Convert.ToInt32(myQueueItem)>50)
    {
        throw new Exception(myQueueItem);
    }
    else
    {
        log.Info($"C# Queue trigger function
         processed: {myQueueItem}");
    }
}
```

3. The preceding Queue trigger logs a message with the content of the Queue (it's just a numerical index) for the first 50 messages and then throws an exception for the all the messages whose content is greater than 50.

Running tests using the Console Application

1. Let's execute the Console Application by pressing *Ctrl + F5*, navigate to the Azure Storage Explorer, and view the Queue contents.

2. In just a few moments, you should start viewing messages in the `myqueuemessages` Queue, as shown here. Currently, both Azure Management portal and the Storage Explorer display the first 32 messages. You need to use the C# storage SDK to view all the messages in the Queue.

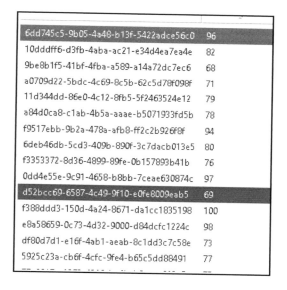

 Don't get surprised if you notice that your messages in `myqueuemessage` are vanishing. It's expected that as soon as a message is read successfully, the message gets deleted from the Queue.

3. As shown here, you should also see a new Queue named `myqueuemessages-poison` (`<OriginalQueuename>-Poison`) with the other 50 Queue messages in it. The Azure Function runtime will automatically take care of creating a new Queue and adding the messages that are not read properly by the Azure Functions:

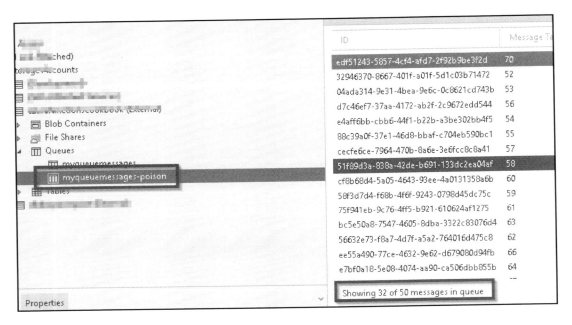

How it works...

We have created a Console Application that creates messages in the Azure Storage Queue. And we have also developed a Queue trigger that is capable of reading the messages in the Queue. As part of simulating an unexpected error, we are throwing an error if the value in the Queue message content is greater than 50.

Azure Functions will take care of creating a new Queue with the name `<OriginalQueueName>-Poison` and will insert all the unprocessed message in the new Queue. Using this new poison Queue, the developers can review the content of the messages and take necessary actions to fix the error in the applications (in this case, Queue trigger).

The Azure Function runtime will take care of deleting the Queue message after the Azure Function execution is completed successfully. In case of any problem in the execution of the Azure Function, it automatically creates a new poison Queue and adds the processed messages to the new Queue.

There's more...

Before pushing a Queue message to the poison Queue, the Azure Function runtime tries to pick the message and process five times. You can learn how this process works by adding a new parameter `dequecount` of type `int` to the `Run` method and log its value.

Handling massive ingress using Event Hub for IoT and similar scenarios

In many scenarios, you might have to handle massive amounts of incoming data, where the incoming data might be coming from sensors and telemetry data, and it could be as simple as the data sent from your Fitbit devices from many end users who use it continuously. In these scenarios, we need to have a reliable solution that is capable of handling massive amounts of data. Azure Event Hubs is one such solution that Azure provides. In this recipe, you will learn how to integrate Event Hubs and Azure Functions.

Getting ready

Perform the following steps:

1. Create an Event Hub namespace by navigating to **Internet of Things** and choosing **Event Hubs**.

2. Once the Event Hub namespace is created, navigate to the **Overview** tab and click on the **Event Hub** icon to create a new Event Hub, as shown in the following screenshot:

3. By default, a **Consumer Group** named $Default is created, which we will be using in this recipe.

How to do it...

We will perform this recipe using the following steps:

- Creating an Azure Function Event Hub trigger
- Developing a Console Application that simulates IoT data

Creating an Azure Function Event Hub trigger

1. Create a new Azure Function by choosing **EvenHubTrigger - C#** in the template list, as shown in the following screenshot:

2. Once you select the template, you need to provide the name of the Event Hub, its `capturemessage`, as shown in the following screenshot. If you don't have any connections configured yet, you need to click on the **new** button:

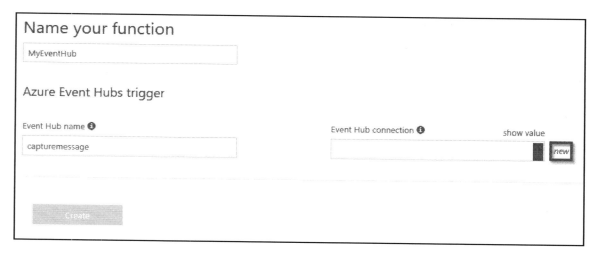

3. Clicking on the **new** button will open a **Connection** popup, where you can choose your **Event Hub** and other details. Choose the required details and click on the **Select** button, as shown in the following screenshot:

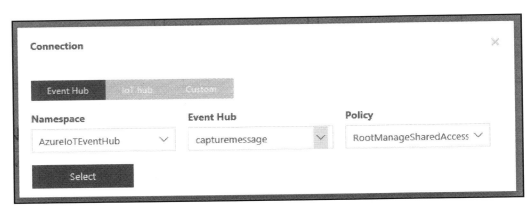

4. The **Name your function** section should look like this after you provide all the details. Now click on **Create** to create the function:

Developing a Console Application that simulates IoT data

1. Create a new Console Application that will send events to the Event Hub. I have named it as `EventHubApp`.

2. Run the following commands in the NuGet package manager to install the required libraries to interact with the Azure Event Hubs:

```
Install-Package Microsoft.Azure.EventHubs
Install-Package Newtonsoft.Json
```

3. Add the following namespaces and a reference to `System.Configuration.dll`:

```
using Microsoft.Azure.EventHubs;
using System.Configuration;
using System.Text;
```

4. Add the connection string in the `App.config`, which is used to connect the Event Hub. This is the code for `App.config`. You can get the Connection String by clicking on the **ConnectionStrings** link available in the **Overview** tab of the Event Hub namespace:

```
<?xml version="1.0" encoding="utf-8" ?>
<configuration>
<startup>
<supportedRuntime version="v4.0"
 sku=".NETFramework,Version=v4.6.1" />
</startup>
<appSettings>
<add key="EventHubConnection"
  value="Endpoint=sb://event hug namespace
    here.servicebus.windows.net/;Entitypath=Event Hubname;
  SharedAccessKeyName= RootManageSharedAccessKey;
    SharedAccessKey=Key here"/>
</appSettings>
</configuration>
```

5. Create a new C# Class file and place the following code in the new class file:

```csharp
using System;
using System.Text;
using Microsoft.Azure.EventHubs;
using System.Configuration;
using System.Threading.Tasks;

namespace EventHubApp
{
    class EventHubHelper
    {
        static EventHubClient eventHubClient = null;
        public static async Task GenerateEventHubMessages()
        {

            EventHubsConnectionStringBuilder conBuilder = new
             EventHubsConnectionStringBuilder
             (ConfigurationManager.AppSettings
             ["EventHubConnection"].ToString());

            eventHubClient =
             EventHubClient.CreateFromConnectionString
             (conBuilder.ToString());
            string strMessage = string.Empty;
            for (int nEventIndex = 0; nEventIndex <= 100;
             nEventIndex++)
            {
                strMessage = Convert.ToString(nEventIndex);
                await eventHubClient.SendAsync(new EventData
                 (Encoding.UTF8.GetBytes(strMessage)));
                Console.WriteLine(strMessage);
            }
            await eventHubClient.CloseAsync();
        }
    }
}
```

6. In your `Main` function, replace the following code that invokes the method that can start sending the message:

```
namespace EventHubApp
{
    class Program
    {
        static void Main(string[] args)
        {
            EventHubHelper.GenerateEventHubMessages().Wait();
        }
    }
}
```

7. Now execute the application by pressing *Ctrl + F5*. You should see something similar to what is shown here:

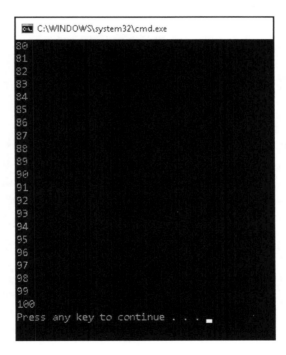

8. While the console is printing the numbers, you can navigate to the Azure Function to see that the Event Hub triggers gets triggered automatically and logs the numbers that are being sent to the Event Hub, as shown in the following screenshot:

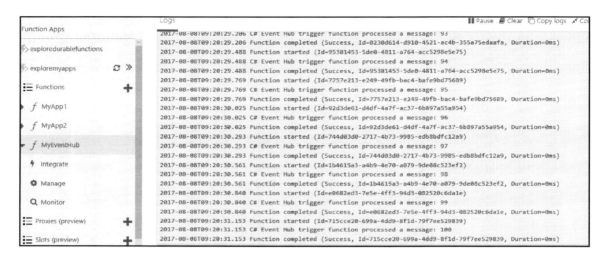

Enabling authorization for function apps

If your web API (HTTP trigger) is being used by multiple client applications and you would like to provide access only to the intended and authorized applications, then you need to implement authorization in order to restrict access to your Azure Function.

Getting ready

I assume that you already know how to create a HTTP trigger function. Download the Postman tool from `https://www.getpostman.com/`. The Postman tool is used for sending the HTTP requests. You can also use any tool or application that can send HTTP requests and headers.

How to do it...

1. Create a new HTTP trigger function (or open an existing HTTP function). Make sure that while creating the function, you select **Function** as the option in the **Authorization level** drop-down:

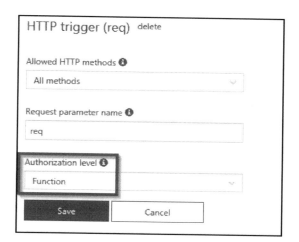

 If you would like to go with an existing HTTP trigger function that we have created in one of our previous recipes, click on the **Integrate** tab and change the **Authorization level** to **Function** and click on the **Save** button to save the changes.

2. In the code editor tab, grab the function URL by clicking on the **Get Function URL** link available in the right-hand side corner of the code editor in the `run.csx` file.

3. Navigate to Postman tool and paste the function URL:

4. Observe the URL that has the following query strings:
   - code: This is the default query string that is expected by the function runtime that validates the access rights of the accessing the function. The validation functionality is automatically enabled without the need for writing the code by the developer. All of this is taken care just by enabling the **Authorization level** to **Function**.
   - name: This is a query string that is required by the HTTP trigger function.

5. Let's remove the code query string from the URL in the Postman and try to make a request. You will get a **401 Unauthorized** error, as shown in the following screenshot:

How it works...

When you make a request via Postman or any other tool or application that can send HTTP requests, the request will be received by the underlying Azure App Service web app (note that Azure Functions are built on top of App Services) that first checks the presence of the header name code either in the query string collection or in the **Request Body**. If it finds one, then it validates the value of the code query string with the function keys. If it's a valid one, then it authorizes the request and allows the runtime to process the request. Otherwise, it throws an error with a **401 Unauthorized** request.

There's more...

Note that the security key (in the form of the query string parameter named `code`) in the preceding example is used for demonstration. In production scenarios, instead of passing the key as a query string parameter (the `code` parameter), you need to add the `x-functions-key` as an HTTP header, as shown in the following figure:

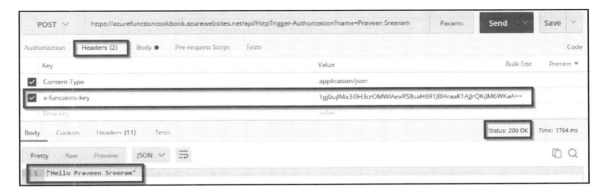

See also

- The *Controlling access to Azure Functions using function keys* recipe

Controlling access to Azure Functions using function keys

You have now learned how to enable the authorization of an individual HTTP trigger by setting the **Anonymous Level** field with the value Function in the **Integrate** tab of the HTTP trigger function. It works well if you have only one Azure Function as a backend web API for one of your applications and you don't want to restrict access to the public.

However, in Enterprise level applications, you will end up developing multiple Azure Functions across multiple function apps. In those cases, you would like to have fine-grained granular access to your Azure Function for both your own applications or for some other third-party applications that integrate your APIs in their applications.

In this recipe, you will learn how to work with function keys within Azure Functions.

How to do it...

Azure supports the following keys, which can be used to control access to the Azure functions:

- **Function Keys**: These can be used to grant authorization permissions to a given function. These keys are specific to the current function to which the keys are associated.
- **Host Keys**: We can use these to control the authorization of all the functions within an Azure function app.

Configuring the function key for each application

If you are developing an API using Azure Functions that can be used by multiple applications, then it's a good practice to have a different function key for every function and generate an individual key for each client application that is going to use your functions. Navigate to the **Manage** tab of the Azure Function to view and manage all the keys related to the function.

By default, a key with the name `default` is generated for us. If you would like to generate a new key, then click on the **Add new function key** button shown in the preceding screenshot.

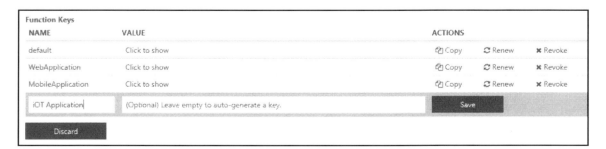

As per the preceding image, I have created the keys for the following applications:

- `WebApplication`: The key name `WebApplication` is configured to be used in the website that uses the Azure Function.

- `MobileApplication`: The key name `MobileApplication` is configured to be used in the mobile app that uses the Azure Function.

In a similar way, you can create different keys for any other app (in the preceding example, an IOT application) depending on your requirements.

The idea behind having different keys for the same function is to have control over the access permissions to the usage of the functions by different applications. For example, if you would like to revoke the permissions only to an application but not for all the applications, then you would just delete (or revoke) that key. In that way, you are not impacting other applications that are using the same function.

Here is the downside of the function keys: if you are developing an application where you need to have multiple functions and each function is being used by multiple applications, then you will end up having many keys. Managing these keys and documenting them would be a nightmare. In that case, you can go with host keys, which is discussed next.

Configuring one host key for all the functions in a single function app

Having different keys for different functions is a good practice when you have a handful number of functions used by few applications. However, things might get worse if you have many functions and many client applications that leverage your APIs. Managing the function keys in these large enterprise applications with a huge client base would be painful. To make things simple, you can segregate all related functions into a single function app and configure the authorization for each function app instead of an individual function. You can configure authorization for a function app using host keys.

Here are the two different types of host keys available:

- Regular host keys
- Master key

Create two HTTP trigger Apps, as shown in the following screenshot:

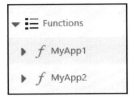

Navigate to the **Manage** tab of both the apps, as shown in the following screenshot. You will notice that both the master key and the host keys are the same in both the apps.

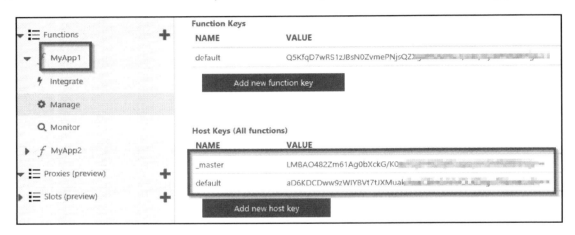

Manage tab of MyApp1

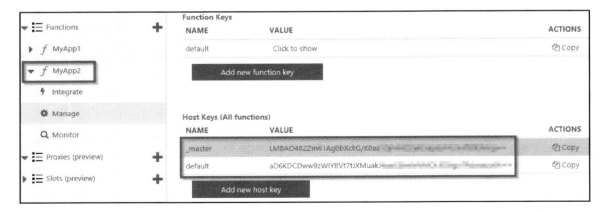

Manage tab of MyApp2

As with the case of function keys, you can also create multiple host keys if your function apps are being used by multiple applications. You can control the access of each of the function apps by different applications using different keys.

You can create multiple host keys by following the same steps that you followed in creating the regular function keys.

There's more...

Renew: If you think that the key is compromised, then you can regenerate the key anytime by clicking on the **Renew** button. Note that when you renew any key, all the applications that access the function would no longer work and would get a **401 Unauthorized** status code error.

Revoke: You can delete the key if it is no longer used in any of the applications.

Key type	When should I use?	Is it revocable (can be deleted)?	Renew	Comments
Master key	When the **Authorization level** is **Admin**	No	Yes	You can use master key for any function within the function app irrespective of the authorization level configured
Host key	When the **Authorization level** is **Function**	Yes	Yes	You can use the host key for *all* the functions within the function app
Function key	When the **Authorization level** is **Function**	Yes	Yes	You can use the function key *only* for a given function

Microsoft doesn't recommend sharing master key as it is also used by runtime APIs. Be extra cautious with master key.

See also

- The *Enabling authorization for function apps* recipe

10

Implement Continuous Integration and Deployment of Azure Functions Using Visual Studio Team Services

In this chapter, you will learn the following:

- Continuous integration - creating a build definition
- Continuous integration - queuing the build and trigger manually
- Continuous integration - configuring and triggering the automated build
- Continuous deployment - creating a release definition
- Continuous deployment - triggering the release

Introduction

As a software professional, you might have already been aware of different software development methodologies that people practice. Irrespective of the methodology being followed, one will have multiple environments such as dev, staging, and production where the application life cycle needs to be followed with these critical stages related to development:

1. Develop based on the requirements
2. Build the application and fix any errors

3. Deploy/release the package to an environment (Dev / Stage / Prod)
4. Test against the requirements
5. Promote the release to the next environment (from Dev to Stage and Stage to Prod)

> Please note that for the sake of simplicity, the initial stages, such as requirement gathering, planning, design, and architecture, are excluded just to emphasize the stages that are relevant to this chapter.

For each change that you make to the software, we need to build and deploy the application to multiple environments, and it might be the case that different teams are responsible for releasing the builds to different environments. As different environments and teams are involved, considering the amount of time that is spent in running the builds, deploying them in different would be more dependent on the processes that different companies follow.

In order to streamline and automate a few of the steps mentioned earlier, in this chapter, we will discuss some of the popular techniques that the industry follows in order to deliver the software quickly with minimum infrastructure.

> In all the previous chapters, most of the recipes provided us with a solution for an individual business problem. However, in this chapter, the entire chapter as a single entity will try to provide you with a solution for **continuous integration** and **continuous delivery** on your business critical application.

The Visual Studio team continuously keeps adding new features to VSTS (https://www. visualstudio.com) and updates the user interface as well. Don't be surprised if screenshots that are provided in this chapter don't match those of your screens in the https://www. visualstudio.com while you are reading this.

Prerequisites

Create the following if you have don't have them already:

1. Create a Visual Studio Team Services (VSTS) account in `https://www.visualstudio.com` and create a new project within that account. While creating the project, you can either choose **Git** or **Team Foundation Version Control** as your version control repository from your VSTS account. I have used TFVC for my project. You can go through the `https://www.visualstudio.com/en-us/docs/setup-admin/team-services/set-up-vs` link to follow the step-by-step process of creating a new account and project using VSTS.

2. Configure your Visual Studio project that you developed in `Chapter` 4, *Understanding the Integrated Developer Experience of Visual Studio Tools for Azure Functions* to the VSTS.

Continuous integration - creating a build definition

A build definition is a set of tasks that are required to configure an automated build of your software. In this recipe, we will perform the following.

1. Create the Build definition template.
2. Provide all the inputs required for each of the steps for creating the build definition

How to do it...

1. Navigate to the **Builds & Release** tab in your VSTS account and click on **New Definition** to start the process of creating a new build definition.

2. You will be taken to the **Select a template** step, where you can choose the required template for your required application. For this recipe, we will choose **ASP.NET Core (.NET Framework)**, as shown here, by clicking on the **Apply** button:

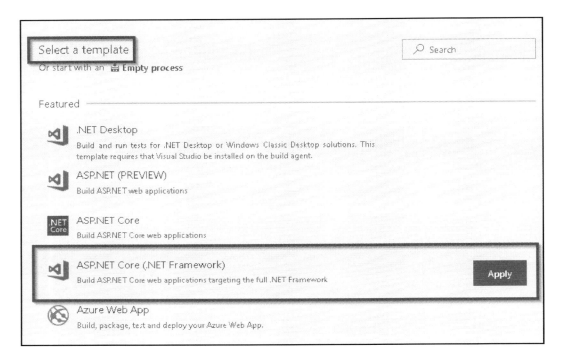

3. The **Create build** step is a set of steps used to define the build template. As shown in the following screen capture, the build definition has six steps, where each step has certain attributes that we need to review and provide inputs for each of those fields based on our requirements. Let's start by providing a meaningful name in the **Process** step, as shown in the following figure:

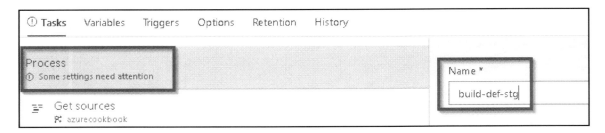

4. Select the **HostedVS2017** option in the **Default agent queue** drop-down, as shown in the following screen capture:

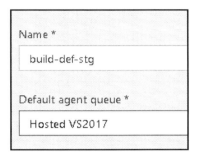

 An agent is a software hosted on the cloud that is capable of running a build. As our project is based on VS2017, we have chosen **HostedVs2017**.

5. In the **Get Sources** step, choose the following:
   1. Select the version control system that you would like to have.
   2. Choose the branch that you want to build. In my example, I have only one default branch.

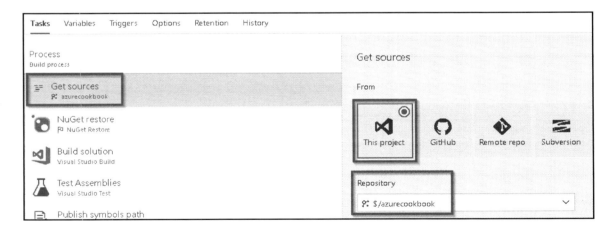

6. Leave the default options for all the following steps:
    1. **NuGet restore**: This step is required for downloading and installing all the required packages for the application.
    2. **Build solution**: This step uses MS Build and has all the predefined commands to create the build.
    3. **Test Assemblies**: This would be useful if we had any automated tests. Test assemblies are beyond the scope of this book.
    4. **Publish symbols path**: These symbols are useful if you want to debug your app hosted in the Agent VM.
    5. **Publish Artifact**: The step has configuration related to the artifacts and the path of storing the artifact (build package).
7. Once you review all the values in all the fields, click on **Save**, as shown in the following screenshot, and click on **Save** again in the **Save build definition** popup:

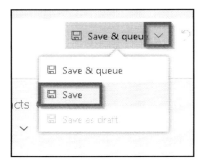

How it works...

Build definition is just a blueprint of the tasks that are required for building a software application. In this recipe, we have used a default template to create the build definition. We can choose a blank template and create the definition by choosing the tasks available in the VSTS as well.

When you run the build definition (either manually or automatically, which will be discussed in the subsequent recipes), each of the tasks will be executed in the order in which you have configured them. You can also rearrange the steps by dragging and dropping them in the **Process** section.

The build process starts with getting the source code from the chosen repository and then downloading the required NuGet packages and then starts the process of building the package, and once the process is complete, it creates a package and stores it in a folder configured for the `build.artifactstagingdirectory` directory (refer to the **Path to Publish** field of the **Publish Artifact** task). You can learn about all different type of variables in the **Variables** tab shown here:

There's more...

1. VSTS provides many tasks. You can choose a new task for the template by clicking on the **Add Task** button, as shown in the following figure:

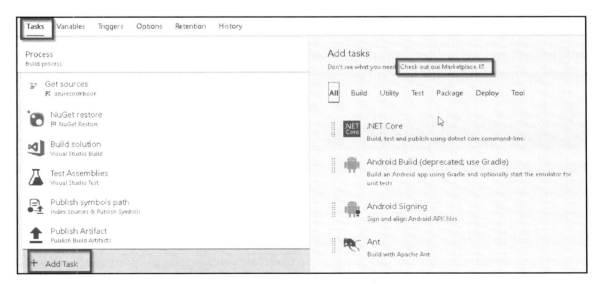

2. If you don't find a task that suits your requirement, you can definitely search for the suitable one in the market place by clicking on the **Check out our Marketplace** button shown in the preceding figure.
3. **ASP.NET Core (.NET Framework)** has the correct set of tasks required to set up the build definition for Azure Functions as well.

See also

- The *Creating a Release definition* recipe

Continuous integration - queuing the build and trigger manually

In the previous recipe, you came to understand and learned how to create and configure the build definition. In this recipe, you will learn how to trigger the build manually and understand the process of building the application.

Getting ready

Before we begin, make sure:

1. That you have configured the build definition as mentioned in the previous recipe.
2. That all your source code is checked in to the VSTS Team project.

How to do it...

1. Navigate to the build definition named **build-def-stg** and click on the **Queue** button available on the right-hand side, as shown here:

2. In the **Queue build for build-def-stg** popup, please make sure that the **Hosted VS2017** option is chosen in the **Agent queue** drop-down if you are using Visual Studio 2017 and click on the **Queue** button, as shown here:

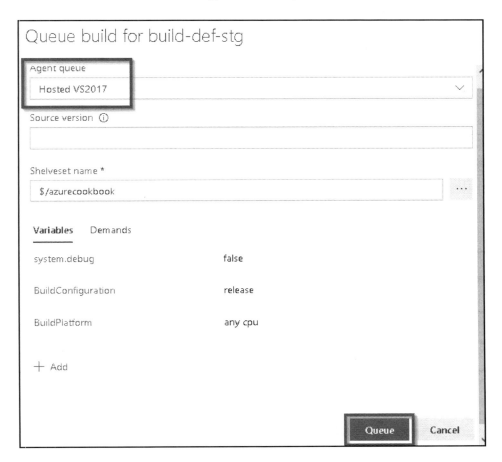

3. After you click on the **Queue** button in the preceding screen capture, in just a few moments, the build will be queued and the message will be displayed as shown in the following figure:

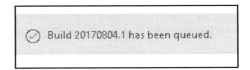

4. Clicking on the **BuildID** (in my case, 20170804.1) will start the process, and it waits for a few seconds for an available agent to start the process, as shown here:

5. After a few moments, the build process will start, and in just a minute, if everything goes fine, the build will be completed and you can review the steps of the build in the logs, as shown here:

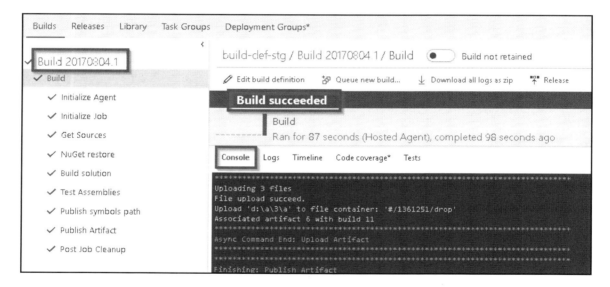

6. In the preceding screen capture, click on **BuildID** (in my case, `20170804.1`) to view the summary of the build, which is also shown here:

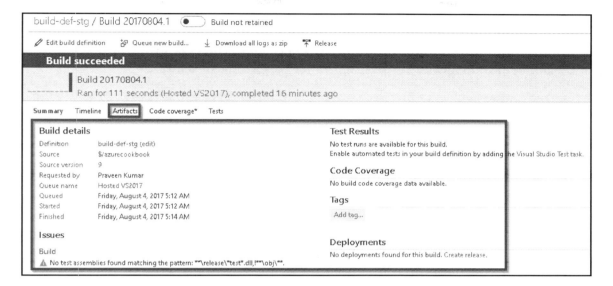

7. If you would like to view the output of the build, click on the **Artifacts** button highlighted in the preceding screen capture. You can (1) download the files by clicking on the **Download** button or (2) view the files in the browser by clicking on the **Explore** button, as shown here:

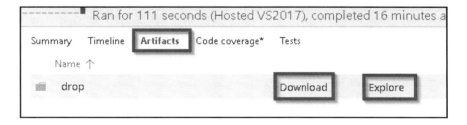

See also

- The *Continuous integration - creating a build definition* recipe
- The *Configuring and triggering the automated build* recipe

Configuring and triggering the automated build

For most of the applications, it might not make sense to perform manual builds in the VSTS. It would make sense if we can configure continuous integration by automating the process of triggering the build for each check-in/commit done by the developers.

In this recipe, you will learn how to configure continuous integration in the VSTS for your team project and also trigger the automated build by making a change to the code of the HTTPTrigger Azure function that we have created in Chapter 4, *Understanding the Integrated Developer Experience of Visual Studio Tools for Azure Functions*.

How to do it...

1. Navigate to the build definition **build-def-stg** that we have created and click on the **Triggers** menu, shown as follows:

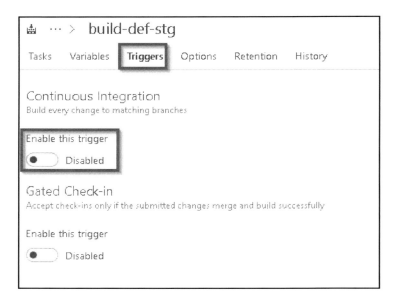

2. Now, click on the **Enable this Trigger** button to enable the automated build trigger. You can also configure the items that you would like to exclude in this step:

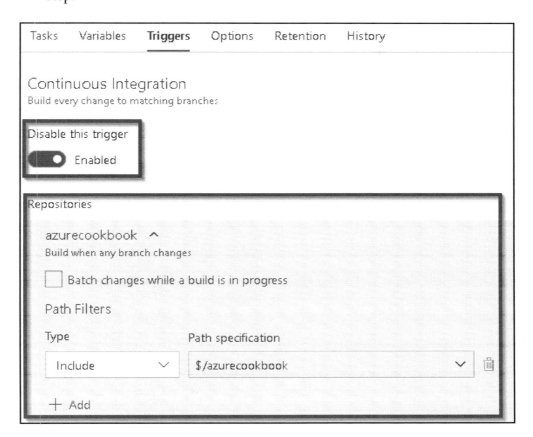

3. Save the changes by clicking on the **arrow mark** available beside the **Save & queue** button and click on the **Save** button available in the drop-down menu, which is shown here:

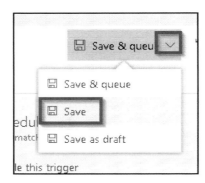

4. Let's navigate to the Azure function project in Visual Studio. Make a small change to the last line of the Run function source code that is shown here. I just replace the word hello with Automated Build Trigger test by, as shown here:

```
return name == null
? req.CreateResponse(HttpStatusCode.BadRequest, "Please pass a
name on the query string or in the request body")
: req.CreateResponse(HttpStatusCode.OK, "Automated Build
Trigger test by " + name);
```

5. Let's check in the code and commit the changes to the Source Version control VSTS. As shown here, you will get a new **ChangeSetId** generated. In this case, it is **Changeset 11**.

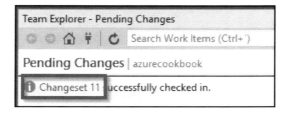

6. Now, immediately navigate back to the VSTS build definition to see that a new build got triggered automatically and is in progress, as shown. Also, note that **ChangeSetId** is mentioned in the **Triggered by** column, as shown in the following figure:

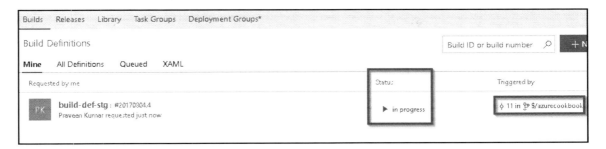

How it works...

These are the steps followed in this recipe:

1. We enabled the automatic build trigger for the build definition.
2. We made a change to the codebase and checked in to VSTS.
3. Automatically, a new build got triggered in VSTS immediately after the code is committed to the VSTS.

There's more...

If you would like to restrict the developers to check in the code only after a successful build, then you need to enable **Gated-Check-in**. In order to enable this, edit the build definition by clicking on the ellipses, as shown here:

In the popup, click on the **Edit** button and then navigate to the **Triggers** tab and enable **Gated Check-in**, as shown in the following figure:

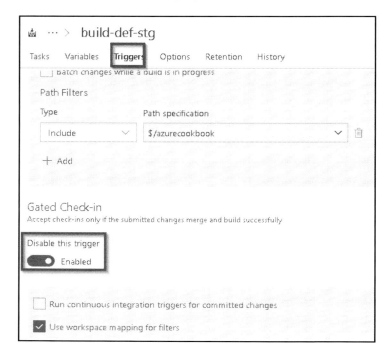

Now go back to Visual Studio and make some changes to the code. If you try to check in the code without building the application from within the Visual Studio, then you will get an alert, as shown here:

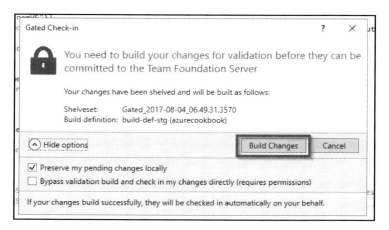

Click on **Build Changes** in the preceding step to start the build in the Visual Studio. As soon as the build in the Visual Studio is complete, the code will be checked into the VSTS and then a new build in VSTS will be triggered automatically.

See also

* The *Continuous integration - creating a build definition* recipe
* The *Continuous integration - queuing the build and trigger manually* recipe

Creating a release definition

Now that we know how to create a build definition and trigger an automated build in the VSTS, our next step is to release or deploy the package to an environment where the project stakeholders can review and provide feedback. In order to do that, first, we need to create a release definition in the same way that we created the build definitions.

Getting ready

I have used the new **Release definition editor** to visualize the deployment pipelines. The **Release definition editor** is still in preview. By the time you are reading this, if it is still in preview, then you can enable it by clicking on the profile image and then clicking on the **Preview features** link, as shown in the following figure:

You can then enable **New Release Definition Editor**, as shown here:

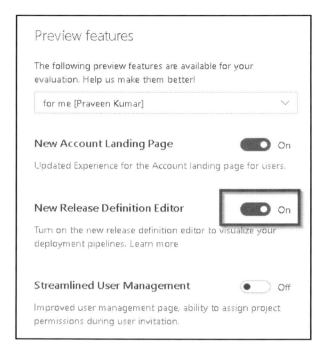

Let's get started with creating a new release definition.

How to do it...

1. Navigate to the **Releases** tab, as shown in the following figure, and click on the **New Definition** link:

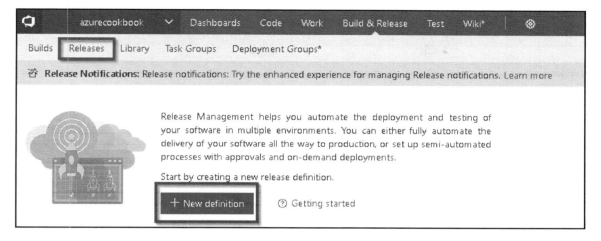

2. The next step is to choose a **Release Definition** template. In the **Select a Template** popup, select **Azure App Service Deployment** and click on the **Apply** button, as shown in the following screenshot. Immediately after clicking on the **Apply** button, a new **Environment** popup will be displayed. For now, just close the **Environment** popup:

3. Click on the **Add** button available in the **Artifacts** box to add a new Artifact, as shown in the following figure:

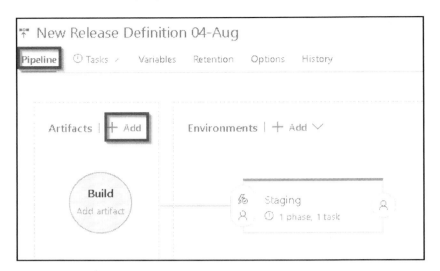

4. In the **Add Artifact** popup, make sure that you choose the following:
    1. **Source type - Build**
    2. **Project** - The team project your source code is linked to.
    3. **Source (Build definition)** - The build definition name where your builds are created.

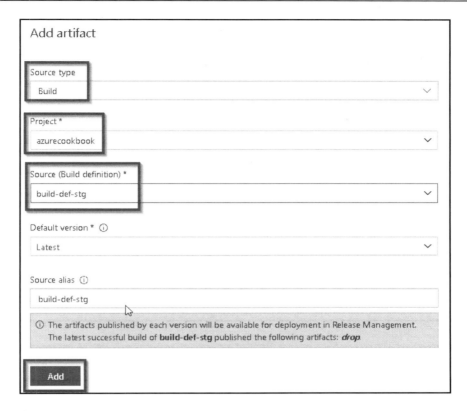

5. After reviewing all the values in the page, click on the **Add** button to add the artifact.

6. Once the Artifact is added, the next step is to configure the **Environment** where the package needs to be published. Click on the **1 Phase 1 Task** link, as shown in the following figure. Also, change the name of the release definition name to **release-def-stg**.

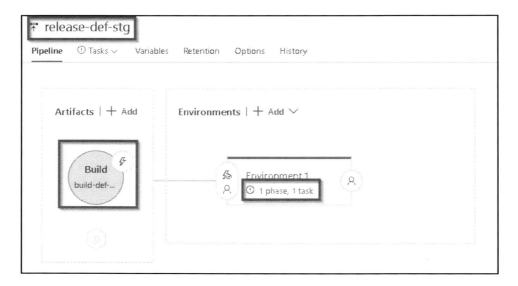

7. You will be taken to the **Tasks** tab, as shown here. Provide a meaningful name to the **Environment name** field. I have provided the name as **Staging** for this example. Next, click on the **Deploy Azure App Service** item.

8. In the **Deploy Azure App Service** step, choose the **Azure Subscription** and the **App Service name** in which you would like to deploy the release, as shown here.

 If you don't see your subscription or app service, refresh the item by clicking on the icon highlighted in the following screenshot.

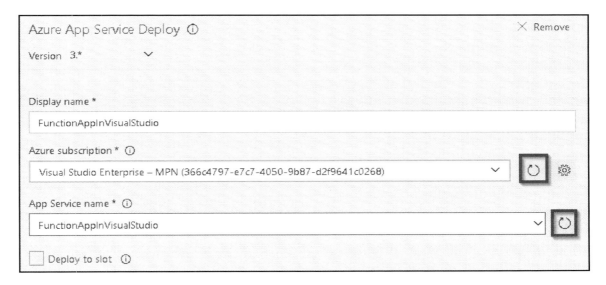

9. Click on the **Save** button to save the changes. Now let's use this release definition and try to create new release by clicking on **Create release**, as shown in the following screenshot:

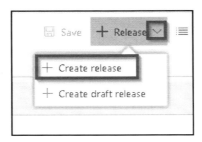

10. After clicking on the **Create release** button, you will be taken to the **Create new release** popup where you can configure the build definition that needs to be used. As we have only one, we can see only one build definition, as shown here. Once you review it, click on the **Queue** button to queue the release:

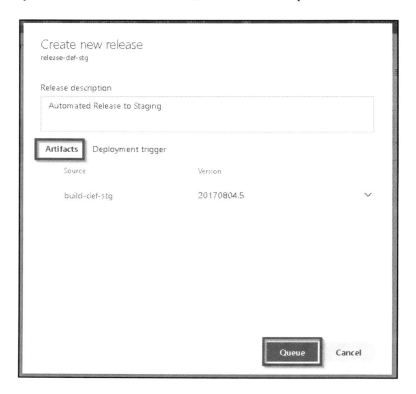

11. Clicking on the **Queue** button in the preceding step will get the package and deploy it to the selected app service.

How it works...

In the **Pipeline** tab, we have created **Artifacts** and an **Environment** named Staging and linked both.

We have also configured the Environment to have the Azure App Service related to the Azure Functions that we created `Chapter 4`, *Understanding the Integrated Developer Experience of Visual Studio Tools for Azure Functions*.

There's more...

If you are configuring continuous deployment for the first time, you might see a button with the text **Authorize** in the Azure **App Service Deployment** step. Clicking on the Authorize button will open a pop-up window where you will be prompted to provide your Azure Management Portal's credentials.

See also

- The *Trigger the release automatically* recipe
- The *Deploying the Azure Function app to Azure Cloud using Visual Studio* recipe of Chapter 4, *Understanding the Integrated Developer Experience of Visual Studio Tools for Azure Functions*

Trigger the release automatically

In this recipe, you will learn how to configure continuous deployment to an environment. In your project, you can configure a Dev/Staging or any other preproduction environment and configure continuous deployment to streamline the deployment process.

In general, it is not recommended that you configure continuous deployment to the production environment. However, it might depend on various factors and requirements. Be cautious and think about various scenarios before you configure continuous deployment to your production environment.

Getting ready

Download and install the Postman tool if you have not installed it yet.

How to do it...

1. By default, the releases are configured to be pushed manually. Let's configure continuous deployment by navigating back to the **Pipelines** tab and clicking on the **Continuous deployment trigger**, as shown here:

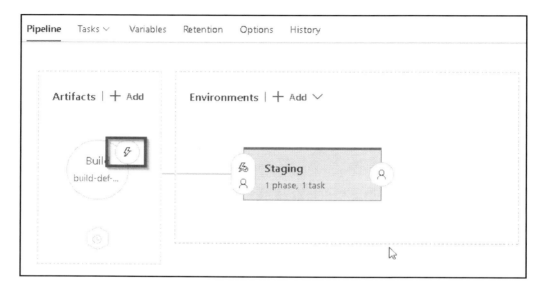

2. As shown in the following figure, enable the **Continuous deployment trigger** and click on **Save** to save the changes:

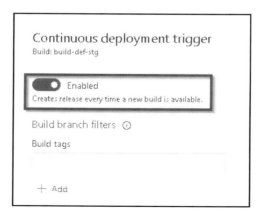

3. Navigate to Visual Studio and make some code changes, as shown here:

```
name = name ?? data?.name;
return name == null
  ? req.CreateResponse(HttpStatusCode.BadRequest, "Please pass a
  name on the query string or in the request body")
  : req.CreateResponse(HttpStatusCode.OK, "Automated Build
  Trigger & Release Trigger test by " + name);
```

4. Now check in the code with a comment `Continuous Deployment` to commit the changes to the VSTS. As soon as you check in the code, navigate to the **Builds** tab to see a new build get triggered, as shown here:

5. Navigate to **Releases** tab after the build is complete to see that a new release got triggered automatically, as shown in the following figure:

6. Once the release process is complete, you can review the change by making a request to the HTTP Request using the Postman tool.

How it works...

In the **Pipeline** tab, we have enabled the **Continuous deployment trigger**.

Every time a build (associated with the `build-def-stg`) is triggered, automatically, the `release-def-stg` release will be triggered to deploy the latest build to the designated environment. We have also seen the automatic release in action by making a code change in Visual Studio.

There's more...

You can also create multiple environments and configure the definitions to release the required builds to those environments.

See also

- The *Creating a release definition* recipe

Index